**St. Louis Community
College**

Forest Park
Florissant Valley
Meramec

Instructional Resources
St. Louis, Missouri

A history of western embroidery

A history of western embroidery

Mary Eirwen Jones

Studio Vista London

Watson-Guptill Publications, New York

Author's note

A full survey of the vast and fascinating subject of western embroidery would fill a series of volumes. Such a project is outside the scheme of this work.

Many valuable books have been written on the various aspects of embroidery, dealing with the subject from aesthetic, technical and national aspects. This volume is put forward in the faith that it will help those who, unable to devote considerable time to the subject, would welcome information dealing in an universal way with the general trends of the national embroideries of Europe, and also of America.

The illustrations have been chosen so as to indicate work characteristic of the nations referred to in the book.

The illustrations from the Victoria and Albert Museum London, numbers 3, 9, 11, 21, 24, 42, 43, 44, 46, 47, 48, 50, 51, 54, 55, 57, 61, 63, 64, 66 are all *Crown Copyright Reserved*.

© Mary Eirwen Jones 1969
Published in Great Britain by Studio Vista Ltd
Blue Star House, Highgate Hill, N 19
Published in the U.S.A. by Watson-Guptill Publications,
165 West 46th street, New York, N.Y. 10036
Library of Congress Catalog Card Number: 77-83369
Set in 10 on 12 Imprint
Printed in the Netherlands
Bound in Great Britain
SBN: 289 79655 5

Contents

Introduction

Embroidery may be described as the art of producing patterns on textiles or on leather in threads of wool, linen, silk or metal by means of a needle.

The art originated in the East where it has retained its eminence in both primitive and cultured life. The study of embroidery in oriental countries is facilitated by the fact that embroiderers still cling to traditions of workmanship and design which were in practice more than a thousand years ago. A survey of the art of embroidery in western countries proves, however, to be a more interesting field for research for therein is reflected the influence of the centuries and of circumstance.

The influence of the embroiderers of the Byzantine empire took root in south-western Europe in and about the tenth century. Embroidery became the handmaid of the early Christian church. In its pictorial representations, it served to unfold religious mysteries to the unlettered masses and in its beauty of form and texture, it enriched ecclesiastical furniture and apparel. For long, workers in the craft sought inspiration from the Near East, an influence which was evident in technique and in design. Byzantine workers, for example, had favoured a design showing a pair of confronting animals or birds separated by the Persian tree of life. The fact that this tree was symbolic of religion to the Persian prophet, Zoroaster, mattered little to Christian workers, who introduced the arrangement freely into work intended for the use of the mediaeval church.

During the crusades in the twelfth century embroidery was used to depict heraldic devices. It is significant that embroidery still retains in heraldic work, as in ecclesiastical furnishings and garments, the ancient and traditional symbolism of colour and of design. Heraldry contributed to the development of embroidery, for much of the present wealth of stitchery in embroidery was occasioned by the complicated nature of heraldic pattern.

As embroidery developed in its range and in its technique, it came to be used widely for apparel and for upholstery. Development of textiles improved the craft but at the same time militated against it, inasmuch that silks and brocades, beautiful in themselves, required no further adornment.

The art of the needle has retained its strength in a mechanized age and is strengthened by the inborn need for individuality, good taste and true feeling. The embroiderer of today is entrusted with the preservation of an art which has been handed down from one generation to the other for many centuries and with the challenge to hand on to succeeding ages something glorious and dignified to enrich the tradition of the fine art of embroidery.

1 The technique of embroidery

Embroidery in a primitive form was known in Europe in Neolithic times. Excavations in early *tumuli* have revealed fragments of cloth woven from linen or fine wool, simply decorated, together with a number of gold and bone needles.

Pliny, when describing the Gauls, states that they were skilful in 'embroidering carpets, in making felt with wool and in using the waste to make mattresses, the invention of which is due to them'. The more northerly countries of Europe developed their arts as the Roman Empire advanced and the simple, artless needlework of these regions became infused with the powerful forces of craftsmanship of the East. As civilization advanced, the art of embroidery developed and the mystic solemnity of the East became evident in the craftsmanship of the West. Nevertheless, the simplicity of western designs and the technique employed in their execution showed an individual virility and charm which were wholly praiseworthy.

A supple thread is essential in all textile crafts. The raw materials used for the creation of the essential textile may be derived from widely differing sources. The weaver in silk and in wool turns to the animal kingdom; the weaver of linen and cotton fabrics finds his resources in the vegetable world while the embroiderer, making use of metal threads and glass discs, can also obtain his material from the mineral world. The importance of the supple thread becomes apparent when it is observed that textiles are grouped according to the manner in which such threads are assembled. A textile can be formed by the continuous manipulation of a single thread, woven simply or woven to create a pattern. Knitting, crocheting and netting are examples of fabrics made in this way. Another method demands the manipulation of two threads; these are crossed at right angles and form the warp and woof of the material. On the basis of this simple process can be built a number of highly skilled combinations. Most textiles come under the range of this grouping, whether they are materials woven on simple hand-looms or intricate tapestries of elaborate design. A further group of textiles demands the use of more than two threads and here a woven foundation textile is essential as a groundwork. On this is worked, according to a preconceived plan, a number of additional threads and to this classification belong those fabrics called embroidery.

Embroidery calls for skill and dexterity in the manipulation of threads and the embroiderer skilled in the craft can draw on a wide range of material, employing all varieties of textiles to his purpose. He enjoys great freedom in technical processes and a great freedom in the use of design. With these established advantages, he enters on his work with assets outside the horizon of workers in contiguous crafts.

Various techniques used in embroidery have prompted classification of the fabrics. A general classification is to divide work into white embroidery and coloured embroidery. This analysis has much to commend it for there exists a close and essential bond between the textile used and the stitches employed upon it. This is most apparent in peasant work of a traditional nature. It is possible to classify coloured embroidery with sedulous accuracy but problems arise when endeavouring to tabulate minutely white embroidery, for the fabrics employed incorporate those ranging from snow-white linen to unbleached varieties.

A method of classification yielding more fortunate results is that which groups embroideries according to the *material* forming the groundwork. In this way more precise decisions can be reached. The divisions are broad and embroideries are divided according to whether the main foundation is of linen, wool, silk, or of gold or silver fabric.

Little progress can be made when one endeavours to classify embroideries according to stitches, because the majority of specimens call into use a variety of stitches and the connoisseur is aware that the greater the number, the richer is the effect of the embroidery.

The basic element of all embroideries is the stitch and it is essential at an early stage to recognize, even if only in a general way, the structure of the stitches used. The stitch is formed by the manipulation of needle and thread. Its size and direction can be pre–determined. Other stitches can be added or attached and at a preconceived angle. The formal character of the design to be embroidered governs to a considerable degree the nature of the stitches used. Authoritative works such as Mrs Archibald Christie's *Samplers and Stitches* deal clearly and illustratively with the formation and history of particular stitches. Suffice it here to say that embroidery stitches can be classified into three main groups. 'Outline embroidery' emphasizes the outline of a design and calls into use such stitches as coral, cable, rope, stem and split stitches. 'Flat mass' embroidery includes inlaid work and couching in which the decorative thread is laid on the surface of the foundation material and is secured in place by a fine thread. Satin stitches, darning, cushion and cross stitches are among those used for this purpose. Into this category comes appliqué work. Material, often of a different texture, is cut out in pattern and attached to the ground material by stitches which form a solid outline. In inlaid appliqué, the pattern is cut out of the ground fabric and decorative material is woven to the back. 'Shading' is introduced into embroidery after the manner of painting. By means of split stitches, feather stitches and others, and by the use of variegated thread, broken masses are given light and shade. Relief is introduced, an effect which is sometimes increased by the use of padding.

Stitches are numerous and represent the development of embroidery through the ages. Flat stitches include the familiar satin stitch, darning, couching and laid work. In these, generally speaking, the stitches are formed so as to lie in parallel lines. Chain stitches include many varieties of chain stitch and split stitches. Looped stitches evolve from buttonhole stitches. Knotted stitches represent a late stage of development; these include French knots, bullion and coral stitches and came to be used extensively when the worker recognized their value as a means of introducing contrast on a smooth fabric or one decorated with flat stitches.

Gold or silver embroideries called for special technique inasmuch as the embroiderer was faced with the necessity of being economical in the use of the expensive metallic thread. The name of purl or purling was given to the metal-wound thread which was placed on the *surface* only of the foundation cloth. At intervals, it was secured in place by small stitches made in a thread of the same or of some contrasting colour. A skilled embroiderer often built up an intricate pattern with the units of these securing stitches. Another method of using gold thread was to draw it tightly to the reverse side of the foundation cloth by a thread which travelled along the reverse side of the design. In this manner, the metallic thread lay along the smooth surface of the fabric and appeared as a flat stitch.

The more skilled gold embroiderers, however, used what was called the Burgundian *lazur* or *nué* process. By this method, gold or other metallic threads were laid along the lines of the design and were secured in position with silk threads. The total effect of gold threads worked in this way bore a close resemblance to woven work. Much of the success of this method was due to the use of a distinct technique in the assembling of the silk stitches. Where light effects were required in the embroidery, the silk stitches were inserted closely; in this way the gold thread showed through. Where a sombre and darkly-shaded effect was sought, the silk stitches were inserted far apart.

The stitches employed in embroidery are reasonably simple in construction but the various classes of embroidery involve the use of intricate technique. This is apparent even in a cursory study of appliqué and cut work where materials of different colours, often embroidered beforehand, are attached to the foundation material by embroidery stitches. It is evident too in relief embroidery where stitches are applied over a raised foundation of wood pulp or of linen weave. Intricate methods are recruited too in the production of pearl or *paillette* embroidery which bears a close affinity to enamel work and where stitches are used to secure pearls, precious stones and semi-precious stones, glass beads and discs or *paillettes* cut out of metal or glass.

During the Middle Ages, embroiderers were limited in their use of technical devices. Embroidery work was usually done, however, on material drawn tightly across a frame. Small fabrics were worked on a circular or tambour frame, an article of Chinese origin. Larger cloths were either placed in a frame after the manner of a high-warp loom or in a frame of the movable type wherein the work was secured into position by means of long stitches. By means of such frames, the worker ensured accuracy in the making of vertical stitches. The frames facilitated the tracing of the outline of the design, enabling the worker to create distinct lines without pulling the foundation cloth out of shape. On the other hand, frames had limiting qualities. When, towards the Renaissance period, frames were abandoned, a variety of new stitches came into being; stitches calling for deftness of fingering and freedom in the manipulation of the cloth.

In the early stages of its development, embroidery had a close affinity with the art of illuminating. Consequently, it was traditional for the great artists of each succeeding age to create patterns for the embroiderer. There was a customary technique of transferring a design on to a cloth. This technique was ubiquitous and appears to have developed but little with the passing of time. Writing his treatise *Il Burato Libro de' Recami* in 1527 the Italian Pagnino gave a minute account of the method of transferring in practice in his day. An account on the same theme described by the French writer St Aubin in *L'Art du Brodeur* shows that a close similarity obtained between the two methods. Indeed, it may be contended that the method described by these writers is widely favoured even to this day.

Fundamentally the process is simple. First, the design is drawn on stiff paper (a heavy tracing paper would be suitable); all lines upon the design are pricked through with a sharp needle. The rough surfaces of these holes are then smoothed down with sandpaper. The paper is placed on the foundation fabric which is stretched across a frame. The paper is then secured in position by pins or small nails. With the aid of a perforated jar, charcoal or chalk powder is sprinkled over the surface of the paper so that it penetrates through the perforated holes. White powder or to give it its technical name – *pounce* – is used on dark material; black pounce is used on light fabrics. The paper is removed from the cloth and the outlines of the design are emphasized directly on to the material with the aid of a brush and water colours.

Embroiderers were dependent on the skill of the dyers in the production of the fabrics on which they worked. In the vat of the dyer were distilled the brilliant and sombre tones of the threads which were essential to a successful needle painting. Dyeing from plants and such natural products as cochineal or chermes is one of the most ancient arts and is coeval with the love of colour evidenced by the cultivation of flowers.

The preparation of colouring threads received the close attention of embroiderers. There is much evidence to indicate that many skilled needleworkers undertook long journeys in order to obtain the more famous recipes for dyeing. Dyers co-operated with them and their manuscripts have survived, indicating the additions and corrections made as a result of their experimenting. One of the most absorbing of such studies is that of the Parisian Jean le Bégue, clerk to the Mint, whose research on the subject occupied him from early in the year 1409 to the close of 1410. He travelled to Italy to study the processes employed in the manufacture of colour. At Bologna, he was fortunate in finding a renowned dyer and fellow-countryman, Thierry, who was employed in the service of the Duke of Milan and who had international experience in the art of dyeing. This enterprising dyer had evolved several new methods of manufacturing colour and it was fortunate for succeeding generations that le Bégue annotated them.

There was a ready interchange of ideas between countries in their efforts to obtain new colours and tones. In some instances, it is true, such recipes were closely guarded secrets. Generally speaking, dyers were open-handed and eager to augment the colours available for the use of embroiderers. Celebrated among the dyers of the fifteenth century was the Frenchman John Gobelins. His name is more usually linked with his workrooms from which evolved for two centuries the internationally famous Gobelins tapestries yet he can lay a claim to fame on account of his more useful dye-works and model workrooms set up on the banks of the Bièvre.

There existed, however, traditional peasant recipes for dyeing silks, wools and yarns. Knowledge of red dyes obtained from the madder plant was brought to Europe by the Turks from the Far East where Turkey-red dyeing was carried on for centuries as a secret process. Yellow dyes were obtained from Persian berries, fustic, tumeric, ebony, wild mignonette, heather and yellow broom. Dark shades of yellow were obtained by placing broom shoots (*genista tinctoria*) in an infusion in which carrots had been boiled or by boiling them in the bark of the crab tree. Leaves of the willow tree yielded orange hues. Black dye was obtained by boiling a brew of well-boiled broad bean pods, sun-flower seeds and the bark of oak or alder. Additional colours were obtained by a process of double-dyeing. Green or violet shades could be obtained by dyeing yellow or red yarn with indigo.

Natural dyes were replaced in 1858 by synthetic dyes. The sheen and beauty, as well as the fastness of colour, of many of the older embroideries is due to the use of natural dyes.

2 *The evolution of embroidery*

Ancient writers refer familiarly to needlecraft. There is, for instance, frequent reference to it in the Book of Exodus. Indeed, attempts at decorating garments were made so early in civilisation that embroidery may well have been the pioneer art of the world, providing the inspiration for drawing, painting and metal crafts.

With the growth of an established order of society, it soon became evident that all ranks in the social hierarchy were attracted by the charm of embroidery. There is ample evidence from the writers of the heroic period that embroidered fabrics were treasured in the Christian and the non-Christian world. Embroidery did not become, as well it might, the perquisite of the bishops and abbots. Kings and princes, queens and courtly ladies were not only attracted by the ornamented fabrics but by the craft of creating them. A halo of mystic solemnity surrounded the early work which was of necessity primitive, depending on coarsely-woven material and large threads for embroidering. Stitches were few and the colours were limited and flat in tint. There was, however, a facility and virility in the design which commanded attention.

The development of embroidery in the mediaeval period was dependent largely on the rise of Christianity and its attendant civilizing forces and upon the revival of classical study. Mediaeval craftsmanship, in all its many virile facets, concentrated its main efforts on service to the church. Subordinate to this, but ever-growing in strength, was an interest in secular and domestic matters. Many influences were brought to bear on the decorative arts. Of these it is probable that none were more powerful than the crusades (1095–1291).

As a result of these holy pilgrimages, oriental and Byzantine influences were extended throughout the western world and they were intensified in those regions where they were already established. Designers and embroiderers, among others, were inspired by the crusades.

There was a contemporaneous development in the technique of embroidery. More stitches were evolved and these were applied with greater precision. Colours were more varied and richer and a definite frankness characterized design.

Those embroiderers who concentrated on religious subjects expressed in their work something of the militancy of the crusaders, evident in the figures and attitudes which they worked. It is possible that such work had, psychologically, a compensatory value for those left behind in the monasteries and nunneries; all were not able to take the sign of the cross and go on a crusade. There was a strong predilection in favour of military figures in design. Among other favourites was St Maurice (who had served as a centurion in a Roman phalanx) and the soldier-bishop, St Martin. A universal favourite was St George who was invariably represented as killing the dragon. The embroideries of several nations portray St Michael in militant attitude overcoming the devil. During the period extending from the twelfth to the close of the fourteenth century, embroiderers portrayed the saints as dressed in armour. Militancy was introduced into biblical scenes as in the grouping of Roman soldiers into prominent positions around the cross in a crucifixion scene.

The crusades had far-reaching effects on all aspects of life. Among the more profound results were those on textiles. It was in 1095 that the crusading spirit of Europe became crystallized, following on the Council of Clermont. Dressed in mediaeval armour, the enthusiastic crusaders hurried forth to the Holy Land. They returned more leisurely, dressed in the rich and luxurious materials of the East, the like of which was unknown to the western world. Moreover, the crusaders brought back many trophies, banners, costumes, pouches, trappings, all of which were adorned with rich embroideries.

On the fourth crusade, Constantinople was seized and plundered. Amidst stupendous pomp, Baldwin, Count of Flanders was crowned. Of particular interest, in relation to the study of embroidery is an account of this coronation written by Robert de Clari.

'After the Count had been accoutred in a splendid panoply, a sumptuously embroidered mantle, jewelled with precious stones, was thrown over him; the eagles embroidered on its outside flashed so brilliantly in the sunlight that it seemed as though the mantle was a blaze.'

Mathew Paris (1200–1259) recorded how the crusaders pillaged rich materials after the Sack of Antioch in 1098. They pillaged to such a degree, says the chronicler, that they became fabulously rich overnight. When the thought of their sinful action weighed heavily on their minds, they sought absolution on their return to their native countries by presenting a part of the spoil to the church. Prominent among these donors was Louis XI (St Louis) of France who endowed the church of St Denis with rich embroideries.

Heraldry (plate 4) received a distinct impetus as a result of the crusades. Embroiderers of the later Middle Ages gave ever-increasing attention to heraldic devices. These were usually embroidered on heraldic bearings and trappings. They also adorned banners and pennons which knights carried in tournaments. As ladies often acted as umpires in such feats of skill, they, too, adopted the custom of carrying embroidered banners. Many of these they embroidered themselves, sometimes depicting on them the figures of the Virgin and also their own portraits. These banners or oriflammes demanded a fair degree of skill for they had to be embroidered in a manner whereby the device could be seen clearly on two sides of the fabric. This requirement led to the development of a special form of embroidery known as *à deux endroits*. The term implied that the back of the embroidery was worked as dexterously as the front.

Fragments only of such heraldic embroideries have survived to the present time (plates 4 and 8). They are however sufficient to show that their creation demanded a high degree of skill. These oriflammes occasioned the creation of new stitches, among them being the *Opus Plumarium* or feather-stitch and *Opus Pulvinarium*, a term referring to powderings of heraldic devices.

As a result of this heraldic trend, embroidery acquired a rich and extensive vocabulary. The term *sablé* was used for small scatterings, *damier* for cross lines or chequers, *ondé* for waved lines, *damassé* for damasked. *Opus Consutum* indicated embroidered work made from small pieces of material sewn together much in the manner of patchwork or placed one piece above the other as in appliqué. The units of such a foundation were often embroidered and the joinings concealed by the laying of a gold cord. The usual practice was to sew the pieces on to the foundation cloth but specimens exist showing that they were sometimes glued on.

Pride of place was given to the working of heraldic motifs on military coats or jupons which were worn on mediaeval armour. Not many specimens have been preserved. A unique and arresting example is the jupon of Edward (plate 14), the Black Prince (1339–76) which was buried with his body at Canterbury. The royal arms are worked on a groundwork of red and blue velvet. Illustrations of mediaeval garments afford evidence that such military coats were in universal use among the royal and noble classes. Flags and banners were similarly embroidered as were also the trappings of the horses. Indeed such records show that the collars of greyhounds bore similar embroidered devices.

Western Europe lagged behind other regions in the creation of beautiful textiles. It is not surprising, therefore, that embroiderers of the mediaeval period endeavoured with the means at their command to create fabrics emulating the rich textiles produced by the older civilizations. Such a desire explains in part the mediaeval vogue for appliqué work. This form had a wide appeal. The technique employed allowed for a slight relief, a characteristic which was to be emphasized strongly later to form the post-Renaissance 'stump' work (see page 39).

Fabrics of this nature came to be used for the costumes of both men and women, which now appeared in a lavishly embroidered form. Ladies of the royal and noble courts, aided by hired needlewomen and by young women of noble blood apprenticed in their households, devoted long hours to the work of emblazoning surcoats and other sumptuous robes. So luxurious did styles of dress become that the Plantagenet kings of England (1154–1485) were obliged to pass sumptuary laws regulating the form of dress. The reign of Richard II (1367–1400) was distinguished for its sartorial extravagance. One of the king's coats was valued at 30,000 marks. France set the acknowledged standard of dress and the noblemen of that country took an especial pride in the magnificence of their robes. Froissart records that the French lords went, under the Duke of Burgundy, on an expedition in 1396 against the Turks 'so richly dressed in their emblazoned surcoats that they looked like little kings'. The richness of such costume proved an encumbrance financially and in a more personal sense, as is testified by a record which maintains that an English nobleman, Sir John Chandos, would have been able to escape from a fatal skirmish at Lussac in 1370 but for the lavish folds of his long robe emblazoned with heraldic devices which impeded him in his course.

A custom prevailed in the Middle Ages of wearing bands on costumes after the manner of phylacteries. They were regarded as charms to preserve the wearer from danger. On them were embroidered figures of protecting saints and the signs of the zodiac. They bore inscriptions and it is significant of a widening culture that Arabic lettering was replacing Roman lettering which gradually fell into disuse.

Accessories of dress grew to be more numerous and more elaborate. They provided fitting vehicles for the display of elaborate embroidery. During the later Middle Ages, it was usual for both men and women to wear pouches or purses hanging from their belts and girdles. They were used for carrying personal requirements and books of devotion. They served as pockets, accessories which were regarded with disfavour at the time. The bags or pouches were embroidered with personal devices and coats of arms. Numerous specimens exist. A careful examination of these will reveal the fact that many of the bags were made from fragments of what were probably sumptuous and much valued garments such as old and hallowed vestments. Other bags were obviously created for the use of the owner from new materials. Intrinsic value as well as sentimental worth was attached to these bags. They were of sufficient value to feature prominently in inventories and in wills. A testament dated 1415 records that Henry, Lord de Scrope, bequeathed to a relative 'a little bag which always hangs round my neck, with a fragment of the True Cross'. Most of these bags were made of velvet or silk. In addition to an embroidered design, they were ornamented with a button or a tassel made of metallic thread or with bells. Other purses were made of leather; these, too, were trimmed with embroidery and were often used for carrying the harness of a sword or a baldric (sword belt) when the owner prepared to take part in a tournament.

Among other accessories, gloves rose to prominence in the later Middle Ages. They had already been in universal use on account of their utilitarian value in hawking and as an essential form of protection for the hand when wearing chain mail. They had a symbolic value also as insignia of office in church and state. Mediaeval England yields specimens of particular interest. In the tomb of St Thomas à Becket were discovered fragments of ecclesiastical gloves. Gloves of similar association are preserved in New College, Oxford. They are, by tradition, the gloves of William of Wykeham who opened the college in 1386. They are of crimson leather and carry an embroidered monogram worked in gold. In the later Middle Ages, men and women adopted the use of gloves for their aesthetic as well as their utilitarian worth; a favourite occupation for ladies was to embroider gloves in silk and gold threads.

As Europe moved forward to higher standards of luxury, textiles were used in ever-growing degree for furnishing and were adorned with fine embroidery. The castle fortress of the early mediaeval period was comfortless and so efforts were made to introduce a measure of comfort and of privacy by partitioning the large draughty rooms and vast halls and by hanging embroidered curtains. The draperies of a room were called a *salle*. They were made in sets and hung on cords and were arranged in such a manner that a great room could be divided into recesses, alcoves and bays. It was the custom in the more ornate of the royal palaces to change these hangings according to the season of the year. Sets of curtains were embroidered suitably for the feasts of Christmas, Easter, Trinity and All Saints. Certain rooms were equipped with permanent curtains, the embroidery of which lent its name to the apartment: the room of the leopards, the room of the golden lilies.

Furniture coverings were made from embroidered cloths. The French term for these – *courte pointeries* – was used universally. Bed furnishings, like those of an apartment, were made in sets and were usually very elaborate. The set included counterpanes, curtains, canopies, headboard and tester complete with three curtains. The beds of the Middle Ages were on a grandiose scale. The enormous Bed of Ware which was capable of holding twelve persons and is now preserved in the Victoria and Albert Museum, London, would not have aroused comment in those days on account of its size for that was commonplace. Inventories and wills afford ample evidence of the existence of such beds and give details of their elaborate furnishings. Kendrick in his book *English Needlework* draws attention to Chaucer's illuminating lines on the beds of the fourteenth century.

> I woll gyve him a fether bed
> Rayed with golde and ryght well cled
> In fyne black sattyn doutremere,
> And many a pylow and every bere
> Of cloth of Raynes to slepe on softe
> Hym there not nede to turne ofte.

Bed curtains were trimmed with cloth of gold and were embroidered with flowers, leopards, lions, serpents and figures.

When kings and noblemen travelled from one estate to another, they took their furnishing draperies with them in great coffers made for the purpose. Inventories relating to these coffers supply detailed accounts of their contents. The lists relating to the draperies of the room prepared at Rheims Cathedral for Queen Joan of Burgundy on the occasion of the coronation festivities refer to furnishings adorned with 'three hundred and twenty-one papegants [parrots] made in embroidery and blazoned with the King's arms'. Others were ornamented with 'five hundred and sixty-one butterflies whose wings were similarly ornamented with the Queen's arms, the whole worked in fine gold'.

The greater portion of the embroidery created in the period including the ninth to the sixteenth centuries was devoted to ecclesiastical purposes. Many of the specimens are lost but it is fortunate that a number of lavish accounts remain. Beautiful fabrics were ornamented with coloured silks and gold and silver thread to serve as furnishings for the church. The ecclesiastical vestments used in the Roman church were numerous and elaborate. The alb (a long, white linen vestment) was decorated with lace and apparels were attached to the front. The stoles falling on each side were richly embroidered and fringed. On his left wrist, the priest wore a maniple and over the alb a chasuble was worn. The cope was an ample cloak ornamented with silks, gold and jewels.

The fine work created on mediaeval ecclesiastical work was an expression of devotion and piety and represents both the labour and delight of all classes of society. The specimens that have been preserved are sufficient to indicate the long years of devoted industry which were spent in making the garments. The vestments of the Church of San Giovanni in Florence are reputed to have engaged the embroiderers for a period of twenty-six years. Dr Rock in his *Ecclesiastical Embroidery* suggests that 'Few persons of the present day have the faintest idea of the labour, the money, the time, often bestowed on old embroideries which have been designed by the hands of men and women, each in their own craft the best and ablest of the day.'

Of the ecclesiastical vestments preserved, copes are in the majority. Many, it is true, have survived in a different form for the ample folds of the garment allowed for its conversion into another garment or furnishing when sections of the original vestment were worn and perishing. Among the more renowned of the early copes are the Syon Cope in the Victoria and Albert Museum, London, the cope at St John Lateran in Rome, and that at Toledo.

The cope was an object attracting the special skill of the embroiderer for this sleeveless vestment was much in evidence when the priest wore it in high ceremonies. It was usually in the form of a semi-circle, a radius ranging from four feet nine inches to five feet. On the wide, semi-circular field both designer and embroiderer could effectively show their skill. Their art was limited by the fact that the vestment had to be worn *around* the figure and that the folds of the garment would inevitably divide the embroidery into spheres of display.

Economy of effort motivated concentration on a *vertical* panel drawn down the centre of the back. On this was focused the central theme of the design. The more usual scenes were those connected with the life of Christ such as the Annunciation, the Birth of Christ, the Crucifixion and the Resurrection. Other scenes were arranged on either side of the vertical panel and they were arranged with recognition of the fact that the scenes were to appear appropriately when the cope was worn. Figures were worked in an upright position and were arranged so that the figures nearest the centre panel confronted. The outer figures were arranged so that they faced the straight edges of the cope and appeared confronting when the garment was worn. The design was thus seen to advantage, for the front edges fell in parallel lines when the cope was worn.

The ground fabric of these copes was varied and was made of rich velvet, silk, brocade or linen. When the foundation fabric was plain, as in linen, it was ornamented freely with silks and gold thread. Figures formed the main theme but the fillings, though subordinate, were worked with care. Into the background were embroidered animals, birds and leaves, the latter being represented on trailing stems. The vine, ivy and oak leaf were among the more popular leaf forms embroidered. Where trailing stems intersected, motifs of birds and the masks of animals were worked.

Much of the embroidery of mediaeval times was the product of domestic industry. In feudal times, it was usual for noble families to place daughters in the castles of suzerains so that they might be educated. In this way, young noblewomen were trained in crafts such as spinning and embroidery. Each chatelaine prided herself on the training given to her maidens. The embroideresses worked in the ladies' bower and as they worked they sang ballads or *chansons à toile* as they were aptly named in France. Early wardrobe accounts reveal frequent entries concerning the embroidery materials used by noble ladies and there also exist early records relating to arrangements for the teaching of embroidery. One of particular interest is that concerning an Anglo-Saxon sheriff of Buckinghamshire named Godric. He granted to a certain woman named Alcuid half a hide of land for a term as long as he was sheriff on condition that she taught his daughter the art of embroidery. Mrs Bury Palliser in her book refers to Denbart, Bishop of Durham, who granted the income of a farm of two hundred acres for life to an embroideress called Eanswitha for undertaking the repair and maintenance of the vestments of the clergy of the diocese.

The monastic workshops and nunneries also produced much beautiful embroidered work. This was devoted mainly to churches linked with the religious establishments but commissioned work was also undertaken and records show that some embroideries were made for the purpose of selling. The products of the monastic establishments have at times been denounced on account of a certain primitiveness which characterized their general style, a feature which marked their secular as well as their religious works. Nevertheless, the monastic embroideries displayed a talent for spectacular descriptive power; they possessed a popular appeal and showed a predilection for narrative.

From the thirteenth to the fifteenth centuries there thrived in the European countries organized embroiderers' guilds. Here England led the way and the continental countries followed closely after. These guilds were active and purposeful and they delivered a strong impetus to the development of embroidery. The value of the mediaeval craft guilds in maintaining a sound general standard of craftsmanship cannot be overestimated. In England, for example, good work in embroidery was maintained in spite of severe national set-backs such as the Black Death (1348) and the Hundred Years' War with France. The weakenings and fluctuations in the sound tradition of needlework were overcome largely through the vigilance of the guilds. The organization of these demanded a long term of apprenticeship, a maintenance of satisfactory work and sound conditions for work such as the rule that all work should be done in daylight. The high standard of

English needlework became traditional and the nation was jealous to preserve this reputation as is evidenced in the year 1423 when the House of Commons presented a petition to Henry VI concerning the poor output of certain embroiderers whose work was being sold at fairs. The value of the guild system was recognized for the petitioners claimed that the poor work resulted from a relaxation of the vigilance of the guilds. It is significant that there was an immediate reaction following on the presentation of the petition; special ordinances were promulgated concerning the use of metallic thread and the guild wardens in London were empowered to search in fairs and to confiscate all work that was below standard.

Across the Channel, the craft guilds were equally active. Interesting documentary evidence relating to the craft guilds of Paris is obtainable from the *Book of Crafts* of Etienne Boileau, provost of the merchants of Paris from 1258 to 1268. He makes reference to the various types of workers including those employed in the textile trades.

Makers of Paris silk and velvets and bourseme en lac.

Spinners of silk using large and small needles.

Makers of thread and silk fringes for the coifs of ladies, pillow cases and the hangings over altars which were made with the needle or with frames.

The tapicers or makers of the tapis sarrasinois or Saracen cloth who say that their craft is for the service of the church or great men like kings and counts.

Reference is also made to men and women skilled in the art of embroidery. Many of them were renowned for their draughtsmanship and two expert women illuminators are named; Dame Margot and Dame Aalès.

The evolution of design and technique

As in all other graphic arts, embroidery reflects faithfully intellectual, psychological, historical and national trends in the lives of the embroiderers. Sources of design are many. They are often contemporaneous, making it difficult to allocate to any one country the honour of conceiving it. The tendency towards unity has increased as the European countries have progressed towards a more unified culture.

Certain fundamental and unifying forces were however prevalent in the Middle Ages. The church, more than any other influence, accounted for this. It emphasized the dualism prevailing in human life. Spiritual powers were at constant war with the sensual and this struggle was revealed to the unlettered in graphic form by means of embroidery. Other intellectual and emotional problems were surging in these times and though these too found expression in needlecraft, they were always relegated a place subservient to that delineating the struggle between heaven and earth.

The draughtsman of the early period of embroidery drew inspiration from many sources and called in the co-operation of the historian, explorer, artist and priest. Sometimes he blended all information and produced an effect which was not altogether unhappy.

The most fecund source of inspiration was the Christian realm, yielding as it did a vast number of incidents from the Bible and an inexhaustible iconography composed of apostles, prophets and saints. Closely linked with this source of supply was that derived from legendary lore both Christian and pagan, the heroes of which intermingled amicably on embroideries. Resulting from early Christian mysticism was a powerful allegorical symbolism. Embroiderers made use of such allegorical representations (plate 2) to serve in their designs. In this way they did an immense service to the church and to the embryo nations of Europe, in that they tutored the masses by means of pictures long before the printing press could serve the purpose. Certain of the embroiderers forsook religious and semi-religious themes and found inspiration in current literature, both verbal and written. Scenes from mediaeval romances were embroidered (for a modern interpretation see plate 71), among the most popular being scenes depicting incidents in the life of King Arthur and his knights. Another rich source of epic romance was Gottfried von Strassburg's *Tristan and Isolde*. Some embroiderers depicted the social life of their time. Such needlework pictures would have been of real historical worth if the embroiderers had not deliberately glamourized people and settings. The love scenes and hunting scenes depicted may have been the highlights of national life in the Middle Ages, but the student of today feels that he could have spared many of the specimens which have survived in order to draw back the veil which tends to shroud the daily life of the commonalty.

Many of the early designs owed nothing to professional artists. Embroiderers relied on patterns easily obtainable from the rural world around them. Geometrical, plant and simple animal forms were used. The living forces of nature had a profound influence on the people. Allied to this was a strong reverence for decorative effects.

This stress on the decorative aspect of embroidery developed as the Middle Ages advanced. Motifs were embroidered with little regard to the use to which the garment or furnishing was put. Designs tended to become more and more biblical; incidents in the life of Christ were favourite themes and Old Testament motifs were less popular than those of the New. Nevertheless, incidents from both sections of the Bible were wont to intermingle in embroidery. The interpretations of scenes were often purely arbitrary; there were marked anachronisms and an established practice of delineating figures in contemporary dress. The new iconography which flourished in the Middle Ages found expression in embroidery and here again there were flagrant anachronisms. St Margaret and St Monica and other such saints intermingle in scenes depicting the Virgin and Child.

The Apocrypha and the Book of Revelations provided useful scenes fraught with symbolism. The four evangelists provided a convenient set in the embroidering of rectangular cloths. The *Agnus Dei* was a favourite theme and was invariably depicted with a halo, a crown and a flag.

Allegorical meanings were attached to many of the animals depicted. The *Physiologus* and other mediaeval bestiaries supplied information relating to these.

Designers of pictorial scenes showed real insight in the grouping of the figures. The main personalities were set against a floral background or one which was subservient and ornamented perhaps with trellis work and inscribed scrolls. Gradually there evolved a strong tradition of placing the main figures within circles or medallions. Rectangular frames were set aside for circular wreaths even when the composition of the design demanded the former. The circular frames became objects of artistic worth in themselves and were intersected with bunches of flowers and ribbon knots.

The prevalence of interlacing band patterns was a legacy from Hellenistic and Roman art. They assumed the form of banderols and inscribed scrolls in the hands of the mediaeval embroiderers. In the fifteenth century the scrolls became ornate, bearing burdens of leaves and of tendrils.

But few specimens show these features in their entirety, for Gothic and Renaissance motifs were prone to intermingle in the long period of transition from one style to another. Moreover, the sources of design were many and they varied in degree of use from country to country. The illuminated manuscripts of the early Middle Ages were copied assiduously; likewise the many samplers worked in each country. These were adorned with flowers, geometrical patterns, scrolls, letters and figures. In this way the samplers provided models for small ornaments as well as stitches.

As embroidery bears a close relationship to the graphic arts in general, designs were inspired by a variety of models. The factors which determined the embroiderer in making a selection were the materials to be employed and the technique to be used. Some of the finer embroideries were inspired by miniatures. Some of the more spectacular specimens emulated stained glass and mosaic work. Needle painting was not an effulgent term for certain embroideries, for the workers (with astonishing excellence) achieved an effect resembling oil paintings and water colours. Other embroiderers, particularly those of the seventeenth century, emulated sculpture and succeeded in their efforts to introduce relief into their work. Present day verdicts on such work are not enthusiastic, for it is recognized that the surface-bound nature of the materials limited the scope of the embroiderers. It is fortunate that so many sought inspiration in the woodcuts and copper engravings which were so popular. The clear cut lines and distinct forms of these were excellent models to copy. Book illustrations provided models when the printing press was invented, as did the work of skilled artists such as that of Hans Holbein the Younger. The eighteenth and nineteenth centuries produced models such as those provided by Mrs Delaney and Miss Linwood while the twentieth century has produced some fine pictorial designs inspired by landscape artists and illustrations in poster technique.

Technique has been inspired and controlled by many factors. Pre-eminent among these are the materials produced by particular districts. Cross stitch embroideries in their many variations were, and still are, prevalent in those flax-producing countries which manufactured linen. The fine linens of Italy called for stitchery of delicate texture (plate 54). Coarse cotton fabrics became vehicles for richly embroidered borders. The more northerly of the European countries have shown a predilection for white work (plate 73). The variety of stitches used resulted in variance of texture. Colour harmonies are often traditional to countries and areas and the student soon learns to classify them in a general way. A common denominator running through time and countries is the virility and charm characteristic of the embroideries, classifying even the humblest specimen as an expression of the aesthetic urge in the human mind.

3 *The embroidery of antiquity*

The origins of this craft of embroidery are lost in the mists of the early legendary history of mankind. By the very nature of the fabric, specimens were lost to posterity and until as late as the twelfth century AD the investigator has to depend mainly on written records.

The aesthetic aspect of needlework followed closely on the utilitarian. The needle was used not merely to join two sections of a fabric together but also to ornament the whole. The limitations of thread contributed in the early stages to the development of technique. The varied surfaces which contribute to the effect in embroidery may have at first been achieved by accident. Threads were originally fine and often weak. To strengthen them, those of weak tension were spun together. Thus there was an early advance towards the production of threads of different texture.

In the earliest phases of known embroidery, these threads were made from wool, flax and cotton. Wool, that of sheep and of goats, was usual in pastoral communities. Flax, yielding linen threads, indicated a high degree of civilization such as that of Egypt (plate 3). Eastern civilizations were familiar with cotton which was conveyed to the Near East by merchant caravans. Silk was the monopoly of China, where it had been known from as early as 1200 BC. It was familiar in the textiles of Persia and of Egypt, however, about the time of the birth of Christ.

Most European countries have taken from an early epoch a practical interest in the production of embroidery. South-eastern Europe led the way, for in late antiquity Byzantium was the centre of textile crafts. Taking inspiration from this fertile source, the Egyptians, the peoples of the Near East, the Babylonians and the Hebrews developed skill in the art of embroidery.

Egypt benefited from her many and advanced industries and perfected the manufacture of fine linen. They honoured the fabric, attributing the invention of flax to their national goddess Isis. Linen was to the Egyptian a symbol of purity, to be assigned an honoured place in all religious rites. The ornamenting of such a fabric therefore called out the aesthetic qualities and highest skill inherent in the nation. The mumming cloths used to wrap the dead were adorned with embroideries in the earliest of historical periods. Geometric motifs prevailed but there was an abundance of pictorial representations. The latter bore all the attributes of Egyptian art, faces shown in profile, the eye represented in full and feet turning sideways, together with the stiffness and immobility which characterized what were supposed to be moving figures. When actual specimens fail to yield sufficient evidence, the student can turn to the numerous early paintings which adorn the walls of royal palaces and of tombs. These give, in surprising detail, representations of the embroideries woven by royalty and the nobility. Preserved at Cairo Museum is an illuminating specimen of some of the earliest applied work made in Egypt. This is the funeral tent of Queen Isi-em-Kebs who succeeded in capturing Jerusalem a short period after Solomon's death in 980 BC. The embroidery is worked on a ground made of hundreds of pieces of gazelle hide adorned with twisted pink leather cord.

An early linen robe obtained by General Reymer while on a French expedition in Egypt carries two square pieces of embroidery on the front and the back of the garment. Similar but smaller pieces of embroidered work are let in on the shoulders. Embroidered panels appear on the sleeves. The linen is yellow, the embroidery thread is brown, and the patterns are based on squares and circles.

Herodotus describes a corselet of Amasis, King of Egypt. 'It was of linen, ornamented with numerous figures of animals, worked in gold and cotton. Each thread of the corslet was worthy of admiration.'

Gold thread was used for embroidery work at an early date. The plates were beaten by hammers into shreds which were later rounded. Moses relates, 'They did beat the gold into thin plates and cut it into wires, to work in the blue and the purple, and in the scarlet and in the very fine linen.' Ancient authors do not refer to silver thread but silver wire was known in Egypt at the time of Thothmes III for remains of it have been found in a tomb in Thebes.

The Jews learnt the art of embroidery when in captivity in Egypt. The Bible contains many and detailed descriptions of embroideries which must have been of an excellent standard of workmanship. The robes of the high priests and the coverings and hangings of the tabernacle bore evidence of the skill of the embroiderers. The Book of Exodus records that Moses arranged for the embroidery of a curtain of fine twined linen for the Holy of Holies. It was decorated with cherubim designed in scarlet and blue and purple. Solomon enhanced his magnificent temple with an azure coloured curtain embroidered with cherubim in blue and in purple. He also arranged for the making of other curtains which were decorated with fruits and with flowers. Representations of animals were excluded.

When lamenting for Tyrus, Ezekiel writes, 'fine linen with broidered work from Egypt was that which thou spreadest forth to be thy sail; blue and purple from the isles of Elishah was that which covered thee.' An account of a veil presented to the Temple by Herod in 19 BC is given by Josephus in his *Wars of the Jews*. He gives the measurements as fifteen cubits by sixteen cubits and says that the fine fabric was embroidered in red and in blue.

The majority of embroidered cloths owned by both Greece and by Rome in the years of their ascendancy were derived from Asia. The fabrics and the patterns were of oriental origin and they represented for the greater part the spoils of victory. Conquered nations would bestow on their conqueror a *toga palmata*, a robe embroidered with palms, symbols of victory. The robe as an insignia of victory was venerated; evidence of this is seen in the moving farewell of the mother of the Macabees as they set forth to battle. 'These maternal fingers spun this thread with which they likewise wove and *embroidered* these garments. May they be either your standards should you vanquish the foe of your God and country or your shrouds should you fall victims to the swords of the faithless.'

Strabo (*c.* 50 BC–25 AD) tells that the Greeks were amazed on the occasions of their warring expeditions into Asia when they saw their enemies dressed in magnificent robes embroidered with silks and gold and jewels. The beauty-loving Greeks were deeply inspired by what they saw and sought to emulate the peoples of the East just as in later centuries the crusaders of more westerly Europe were influenced by the culture and civilization of the Near East. Imitation of Asiatic fabrics and embroideries followed closely on the conquering expeditions. Alexander the Great, gloating over his possession of the richly embroidered Tent of Darius, commissioned the skilful Cypriotes to make him a conqueror's robe.

Greek interest in fine fabrics and the ornamenting of these was long established. Homer makes frequent reference to embroidery. He states that expert embroideresses were brought from Sidon to Troy, that Helen of Troy embroidered a picture representing the Trojan wars and that Ulysses wore a mantle embroidered with a hunting scene. Aeschylus (525–456 BC) also described the heroes as wearing embroidered robes. Prominent in Greek literature is the legend which tells how Minerva, skilled in the art of weaving, was indignant at the effrontery of Arachne who pitted her skill against that of the goddess, and changed her into a spider. The tale is told in Ovid's (43 BC–57 AD) *Metamorphosis* and has often been the subject of English verse.

> Straight to their posts appointed both repair,
> And fix their threaded looms with equal care.
> Around the solid beam the web is ty'd,
> While hollow canes the parting warp divide.
> Thro' which, with nimble flight, the shuttles play,
> And for the woof prepare a reedy way.
> The warp and woof unite – pressed by the toothy slay;
> Thus both, their mantles button'd to their breast,
> Their skilful fingers ply with willing haste,
> And work with pleasure, while they cheer the eye
> With glowing purple of the Tyrian dye;
> Or, justly intermixing shades with light,
> Their colourings insensibly unite.
> Then threads of gold both artfully dispose,
> And as each part in just proportion rose,
> Some antique fable in their work disclose.

Many of the finer embroidered cloths of Rome were not manufactured at home but were imported. They were as a result very costly. Virgil (70–19 BC) in his *Æneid* relates how the son of Anchises gave brave Cleanthes a magnificent robe decorated with purple borders. The richness of the pattern may be inferred from the words: 'Upon the web was embroidered the son of Tros in a forest, javelin in hand, chasing a fleeting hart. He burns with zeal and pants for breath, when suddenly, Jove's bird, swooping from the summit of Mount Ida, seizes him in its claws and bears him away to the heavens.'

According to documentary evidence, such hunting scenes, coupled with those representing the exploits of the gods and goddesses, were usual on the larger and more spectacular fabrics of the Roman Empire. On clothing, designs were simpler; motifs of birds, flowers and trees were usual.

Documentary evidence is of especial importance when discussing the embroidered garments of the Roman Empire, as no actual specimens survived. It is clear that the custom of wearing embroidered garments became so extravagant that Diodorus Siculus declares that the Locrian legislator, Zaleucus (seventh century) promulgated a law whereby courtesans were not entitled to wear such robes. Motives of economy rather than personal taste may have inspired the opinion of the Emperor Alexander Severus, who declared a preference for plain rather than embroidered linen. According to his biographer 'If linen cloths are made of that material in order that they may not be at all rough, why mix purple with them. To interweave gold with linen is madness for this makes it rigid as well as rough.'

Judging from the wall paintings on the catacombs the early Christians appear to have been interested in embroidery and there existed a tradition that the Virgin Mary embroidered a veil for herself after the visitation of the Angel Gabriel. The early Christians were subject to so many hardships and persecutions that the embroideries on ecclesiastical garments must have been made with great difficulty.

The courts of the Roman emperors displayed costly embroideries. The exact value of these ornamented cloths is difficult to ascertain at the present time, but M. Eugène Muntz's theory is that the great velarium commissioned by Nero as a hanging for the Colosseum was not a tapestry-weaving but an embroidery. It showed Apollo driving his steeds across the starry sky, and such rich, gaudy representations were characteristic of Roman art in general. From the third century onwards, Roman emperors dressed themselves in togas made from rich fabrics and embroidered so magnificently that they resembled oriental potentates.

The Near East was a fecund source of inspiration and Rome did much to emulate Byzantium. When Constantine established it as a seat of government, he was able to command much of the opulence of Asia. This was of immeasurable importance in the development of textiles and of embroideries. Francisque Michel refers to these in his authoritive *Récherches sur les Etoffes de Soie*. Fabrics were made in Byzantium in imitation of those imported from the East. Designs were varied, including flowers, palms and shrubs, fruits, unicorns, basilisks, lions, tigers, elephants, peacocks and eagles. The names recorded in Byzantine records became usual currency in the vocabulary of textiles in the Europe of the Middle Ages. *Virgata* implied a fabric or ornament with stripes; *stuculata* with diamond tracings; *pallia cum rotis* referred to medallions which were much in use. *Cum bestis et avibus* referred to fabrics decorated with beasts and birds. *Cum historia* was used for designs referring to mythology and to the Bible. Large fabrics were hung in public buildings. Cloths were heavy and were suitable vehicles for the elaborate and weighty embroideries of Byzantium.

Christian devotion expressed itself in the embroidering of cloths for the use of churches. The altar cloth of St Sophia was described by Paul the Silentiary as being embroidered. The design showed the figure of Christ robed in purple tunic and golden mantle of dazzling effulgence; in his left hand he held the Book of the Gospels. His right hand was stretched forth and on either side, clad in white, was St Peter with the Book of Holy Writ and St Paul with a gold staff surmounted by a cross. Along the borders were representations of miracles and diverse incidents of sacred history amongst which the flattering artist had depicted Justinian (483–565) distributing alms to the churches.

There was a marked deterioration in taste when sacred scenes were used to decorate secular robes. Biblical subjects were interspersed with motifs representing wild animals and hunters. Such a practice called down upon the wearers the anathema of the early bishops, who denounced the populace for wearing the scriptures on their backs instead of on their hearts. Some of the more ambitious of the Byzantine embroideries had a rigid quality, for the workers strove after effects in solid relief. A few of the early Byzantine embroideries have been preserved. Some were exhumed from a tomb of the third century AD. So highly were Byzantine embroideries valued in Europe, however, that they were copied very carefully and their influence prevailed far into the Middle Ages.

Byzantine artists took refuge in south-eastern Europe following on disturbances in Constantinople. Athanasius (*c.* 296–373), in his *Liber Pontificalis*, describes how many experienced embroiderers found refuge and occupation in Rome. The Greeks also bene-fited from the Byzantine migration and it was largely due to them that much of the Byzantine skill was preserved in Europe.

An embroidered cloth dating from the period of the Byzantine domination in Europe was exhumed from the tomb of Gunther, Bishop of Bamber. The Emperor Constantine (272–337) is portrayed on it as ruler of heaven and earth. He is shown as receiving hom-age from two queens, who represent the two Romes. The proportions of the figures and the exactness of workmanship are striking features of this embroidery preserved at Ratisbon.

The triumph of Mohammedanism in the seventh century contributed fresh life to textiles at a time when the glory of Byzantium was passing. Oriental fabrics were rich, oriental embroideries were varied. The latter were not confined to woven fabrics but were used ingeniously to decorate leather, shaped into saddles, harness, scabbards and boots. The nomadic Arab delighted in embroidering his tent. It is recorded that Haroun-el-Raschid sent a present of an embroidered tent and embroidered textiles to Charle-magne in 802. Rich embroideries were hung in the Kaaba in Mecca. Devotion and wealth were expressed by hanging heavy embroidered cloths on the tomb of Mohammed. So numerous were these textiles at one time that the fabric of the building was endangered by their number and weight. Green, as the symbolic colour of the prophet, was used for the ground and coloured threads were used to embroider passages from the Koran and to inscribe the prayers of Islam. The influence of the Near East was intensified at the time of the crusades when Europeans came into direct contact with the older and more luxurious civilization.

Embroidery in these early ages was a means of teaching religious faith to the unlettered. Hence its wide appeal in all countries and to all classes of society.

4 English embroidery

Opus Anglicanum

An early British barrow opened in Yorkshire brought to light a fragment of linen believed to have been woven in almost pre-historic times. The *London Chronicle* of 1767 contains an account of the opening of a Scandinavian barrow near Wareham in Dorsetshire and relates the discovery of a piece of gold lace. Boadicea is reputed to have worn a beautifully embroidered mantle.

The impetus to the development of early textiles in the Roman period was probably considerable. When St Augustine arrived in Kent (597), he is accredited with carrying a banner embroidered with the figure of Christ. Several authorities have stressed the resemblance between the embroidery done in Egypt during the time of the Roman occupation and that done in England in the seventeenth and eighteenth centuries. It is possible that the foundations for such traditional designs were laid in England in the time of Julius Caesar. If, however, embroiderers in England did ornamental work of this nature under the Romans, time and circumstances have obliterated any and all specimens and documentary evidence is lacking.

There exists a theory that during the Anglo-Saxon and Danish invasions, the art of embroidery was fostered in Britain through the teachings of captive women who had been torn from their homes in the more southerly parts of Europe. Decided advance was made in the art of embroidery under Saxon rule, and Anglo-Saxon women were acclaimed internationally for their craftsmanship. St Aldhelm, an eminent scholar of the seventh century, who was abbot of Malmesbury and later bishop of Sherborne, made eulogistic reference in a poem to the tapestry work and embroidery in which the women of his time were engaged.

The greater portion of the embroidery of this early period was devoted to ecclesiastical purposes. Many specimens are lost entirely but there exist detailed accounts of sarks (shirts) and of tunics embroidered with gold threads and coloured silks. These garments were worked in the seclusion of convents by pious nuns. They were also made in the courts of kings and of the nobility by ladies who devoted their leisure to embroidery. References to such embroideresses are numerous. Emma, who was in turn the queen of Ethelred the Unready (? 968–1016) and of Canute, was renowned for her ability in designing and embroidering ecclesiastical vestments and church furnishings. William of Malmesbury describes Edgitha, the wife of Edward the Confessor, as a 'perfect mistress of her needle'. She embroidered the mantle which the king wore at his coronation. An earlier embroideress was St Etheldreda who lived in the seventh century. She was the first abbess of the convent at Ely and her influence was far-reaching. She made an offering to St Cuthbert of an embroidered garment which she had ornamented with gold thread and precious stones.

St Dunstan (924–988), Archbishop of Canterbury, was renowned as the designer of embroideries for noble ladies. According to one record, he is said to have gone daily to the bower of a certain Lady Ethelwynne in order to superintend the embroidering of his designs. One day the monk made a strange noise, calling to aid his powers of ventriloquism and his skill with an Aeolian harp. Frightened by the sound, the ladies fled in abject terror. When the monk's trick was discovered, he was banished from court. He was denounced as a wizard and ducked in a pond to prove his innocence according to the accepted method of trial for witchcraft. His innocence was proved but subsequently St Dunstan was represented on old missals and psalters as a figure playing on an Aeolian harp.

Embroidery was recruited for more general use. The battle standard used by King Alfred (871–900) is said to have been richly embroidered; it bore the symbol of a crow. The banner was reputed to be the work of Danish princesses. Another Danish banner embroidered with a raven, the work of Ragnar Lodbrog, was, according to legend, endowed with miraculous power; the bird could foretell the outcome of battle by the position of its wings.

The ladies of the court of Edward the Elder (d. 923), were renowned for their skill in many crafts. William of Malmesbury records that the king ordered his children while still young 'to give their whole attention to letters and afterwards employed them in the labours of the distaff and needle.' The stole and maniple of St Cuthbert preserved in Durham Cathedral (plate 5) are said to represent the work of Aelfled, queen of Edward the Elder. Edgitha, queen of Edward the Confessor – she whom William of Malmesbury termed 'the perfect mistress of her needle' – embroidered a rich vestment in gold for the abbot of St Requier in Picardy.

Matilda, queen of William the Conqueror, was greatly skilled in embroidery. Her gifts to churches were numerous. She gave to the Church of the Holy Trinity at Caen a tunic which was described as the work of one Alderet of Winchester. To the same church, Matilda gave her gold embroidered mantle so that it might be converted into a cope. She also presented this church with her golden girdle for the purpose of suspending the lamp before the high altar.

The embroidery usually associated with the name of Queen Matilda is that known as the Bayeux Tapestry. This work is an embroidery not a tapestry. Theories have been put forward that the work is not that of Matilda, the wife of the Conqueror, who died in 1087 but of the Empress Matilda, wife of Henry v, Emperor of Germany, who later married Geoffrey of Anjou; the Empress Matilda was the grand-daughter of William the Conqueror. Kendrick in his *English Needlework* thinks that it is safe to assume that the designers of the work were of the same race as the Normans and sympathetic to their conquest. He weighs the evidence fairly and expertly and points out that to argue that the work was embroidered half a century to a century later was to imply that the workers had an historic sense, and an observation of local detail which was almost super-human.

The historical value of this great epic embroidery is immeasurable. M. de Ronchaud in *La Tapisserie dans l'Antiquité* emphasizes the close resemblance between the classical embroideries representing the siege of Troy and the Bayeux Tapestry. The famous needlework preserved at Bayeux probably represents the work of a considerable period of time. Worked on a band of linen two hundred and seventy feet long and twenty inches wide, it records vividly the stirring scenes of English history from the accession of Edward the Confessor to the defeat and downfall of Harold. The panel abounds in historical data. On it are embroidered figures dressed in armour, ships, horses, weapons.

One thousand two hundred and fifty-five figures are worked on the linen.

The standard of workmanship on the panel is not high and it cannot be accepted as representing the highest skill of the time; earlier work is far less crude. The workers, however, may have been in no sense ambitious. It is probable that they would have been astounded by the interest and value placed on their work by subsequent ages. The 'tapestry' to them was a means of whiling away their enforced leisure in captivity at Caen.

The name tapestry has clung to the work, which is in reality an embroidery in which worsted threads are couched on the surface of the linen. These are held in position by cross stitches worked over the couched threads and inserted into the linen background. The colours were selected without any thought of harmony, the figures are crudely drawn and it is significant that it was thought necessary to embroider inscriptions to interpret the scenes. With all these deficiencies, however, the Bayeux Tapestry remains an object of perennial charm.

The Middle Ages

Britain has the distinction of excelling over other European countries in the art of embroidery in the period extending from the twelfth to the fourteenth centuries.

Old chronicles invariably refer to the embroidery as 'English work', a term which occurs frequently in the inventories of most European nations. The embroideries referred to include domestic and secular garments and furnishings as well as those intended for ecclesiastical use.

It has been suggested that the term *Opus Anglicanum* may have had a special connotation with reference to a particular style in design or technique. Generally speaking, however, the term is interpreted as referring to work done *in England* – such work was recognized as possessing a high quality of design and of workmanship (plate 7).

Circumstance contributed to the high standard of work attained. During the period under discussion, the graphic arts flourished in Britain and embroiderers were caught up in the high tide of excellence which also bore skilled illuminators, workers in wood and in metal, in stone and in ivory.

The demand for *Opus Anglicanum* was high, for the fame of the embroiderers was widespread. Old inventories and accounts show that much of the embroidery work of mediaeval England was commissioned. Mathew Paris records that Pope Innocent IV learnt in the year 1246 that England was the source of certain sumptuous vestments. He exclaimed, 'Truly, England is our garden of delight; in sooth, it is a well inexhaustible and where there is great abundance; from thence much may be extracted.' He sent official letters to the abbots of certain of the Cistercian monasteries in England and asked them to send to Rome for his use vestments embroidered in *Opus Anglicanum*.

The inventories of the papal treasury provide the most valuable information concerning specimens of *Opus Anglicanum*. The worth of English embroidery can best be assessed by the predilection of popes for this variety of work. So enamoured of this type of embroidery was Pope Urban IV (1261–1264), that he employed an English embroiderer skilled in gold work. Pope Nicholas II (1277–1280) gave to the Basilica of St Peter in Rome two chasubles and a cope decorated with English embroidery. Nicholas IV and Boniface VIII gave English vestments to churches of their choice. Of special interest as surviving to the present time is a cope presented by Clement V (1305–1314) to the cathedral at St Bertrand-de-Comminges. Clement VI (1342–1352) gave to the Basilica of St Peter a gift of English embroidery and in 1462 Pope Pius II presented to Piacenze *Opus Anglicanum* which is treasured to this day as one of the most perfect examples surviving from the fourteenth century.

Opus Anglicanum treasured in Europe and America at the present time includes ecclesiastical vestments of many kinds. Copes, however, are greatly treasured inasmuch as in them may be traced the cycles of development which occurred in the period.

The earliest cycle revolves round the period 1250 to 1275. Designs show mainly figures of saints or representations of biblical events which are enclosed in circles or medallion- and are surrounded with garlands; groupings are arranged in concentric circles. Specimens of this period are not numerous and are composed mainly of fragments such as those belonging to the vestments of Bishop Walter Cantelupe.

The next cycle includes the period of time extending from about 1275 to 1325. The most famous specimen is the splendid cope of Syon (see page 29); almost as impressive is the Daroca Cope in the Museo Arqueológico in Madrid. A greater freedom characterizes design. Scenes are no longer confined in circular but in Romanesque quatrefoils which are sometimes interlaced.

The final cycle occupies the greater part of the fourteenth century. In it the finest work was done (plate 6). Famous copes of this time include those of Piacenza, Bologna, Toledo and the Lateran Basilica. Designs are now arranged under Gothic arches and are set out in two or three concentric circles; scenes are separated by architectural columns or by variations of them in the form of tree trunks, enlaced ribbons and stems of flowers.

Specimens of English embroidery of the Middle Ages cannot be classified into local schools. There is a certain uniformity of design and of technique which obliterates most evidence as to locale. Workers did not record their names as a rule but by means of old records it is possible to trace the names of many of the embroiderers. Wardrobe accounts of the reign of Henry III give the names of male embroiderers, among them Adam de Bakeryne, John de Colonia and Alain de Basinge. Women's names include those of Mabilia of Bury St Edmunds and Rose de Bureford.

In emphasizing the English quality of the embroidery of the time, one must give full value to foreign influences. Artists and craftsmen travelled far; there was frequent movement from one monastic or conventual settlement to another. Royal marriages bound countries together and the Roman Catholic Church established European unity. As a result of this, English embroiderers must have improved their skill and derived fresh inspiration from workers in France, Italy, Spain and other European countries.

More than one person was usually employed in the embroidering of a fabric; the size of the work and fineness of the embroidery called for co-operative work. An altar frontal presented to Westminster Abbey in 1271 had occupied four women for four years. Vestments of a church in Florence had occupied a number of persons for twenty-six years.

Characteristic features of English embroidery are the representations of animals portrayed realistically, the predilection for birds of every species, the abundance of foliage, cherubs on wheels and numerous angels equipped with wings suggestive of a peacock's feathers. Figures are numerous and well modelled and special care is given to accurate proportions of the body. This is particularly true of earlier work; in the later Middle Ages the rules became relaxed and perspective was ignored.

Stitches are even and of an astonishing fineness yet there is an arbitrary selection of colours. Faces are worked in split stitch arranged in such a way that an effect of relief is produced. So well is this effect achieved that for long a theory prevailed that mediaeval embroiderers had been skilled in producing relief by resorting to the use of a small hot iron which was pressed against certain surfaces of the face and the body of the embroidered figures. Close examination has shown that the embroiderers achieved their remarkable results by means of stitchery only. The spiral chains are distinguishing stitches of early English embroidery.

Opus Anglicanum appears at its best in the embroidering of church vestments. Fragments of silk vestments taken from episcopal tombs at Worcester Cathedral are now housed in the treasury of that edifice and in the British Museum and the Victoria and Albert Museum. The remains represent portions of stoles and of maniples in red silk. The designs include those of apostles and kings worked in gold thread.

The finest cope of this golden age of English embroidery is that known as the Syon Cope preserved in the Victoria and Albert Museum. The cope receives its name from Syon House, Isleworth, the home of Bridgettine nuns. The date of its working is unknown but on the evidence of the armorial bearings which border the vestment it is conjectured that it was embroidered in or near Coventry.

The cope is of linen; the embroidery is worked in coloured silks and gold and silver thread. It measures four feet eight inches wide and it is nine feet seven inches in length. The design indicates that it was worked in the second of the great cycles of English embroidery. Interlacing quatrefoils cover the ground-work. These quatrefoils are covered with red silk; the intervening spaces are covered with green silk and are decorated with six-winged angels standing on wheels.

The central quatrefoil shows a crucifixion scene where the body of Christ is embroidered in silver and cloth of gold. The Virgin stands beside the cross; she is dressed in a green tunic and golden mantle. On the other side of the cross stands St John, embroidered in gold. A quatrefoil above this central scene shows Christ with the Virgin and another below shows St Michael overcoming Satan. Other quatrefoils depict scenes in the life of Christ, of the Virgin and of the apostles. It is most probable that the cope has been cut down from its original size. An edging in a cross stitch design attached to the cope is of later date. Likewise of later date is the heraldic orphrey.

The cope itself is worked in fine stem stitch with the faces and couching worked spirally.

This vestment has an interesting history. It probably remained in Isleworth from the time of Henry v to Elizabeth. Following on many vicissitudes in Flanders, France and Portugal, it returned to England in the mid-nineteenth century and finally reached a safe harbour in the Victoria and Albert Museum.

Chasubles decorated with English embroidery have also been preserved. Specimens in red silk, beautifully ornamented with silks, gold leaves and pearls, were discovered in the tomb of Hugh Pudsey, Bishop of Durham who died in 1194.

Some magnificent chasubles of the mediaeval period are preserved in the Victoria and Albert Museum. One of blue satin carries barbed quatrefoils with biblical scenes worked in silver and coloured silks. The background is embroidered with scrolls, griffins and lions.

A red brocaded chasuble of fifteenth century date in the same museum shows scenes in the life of Christ together with a series of unusual designs showing male and female saints beneath canopies of Gothic arches.

Mitres were embroidered in *Opus Anglicanum*. St Thomas à Becket, martyred at Canterbury in 1170, wore an embroidered mitre and stole. The fragmentary remains of a mitre worn by Bishop William of Wykeham (1367–1404) preserved in New College, Oxford, show embroidered work enhanced with silver thread and jewels.

Altar frontals and dossals were also embroidered. Designs on these were placed in an upright position and did not radiate as in copes. The crimson velvet Nevill frontal in the Victoria and Albert Museum dates from the late fourteenth century, the beginning of the debased period of *Opus Anglicanum*. Groups of figures appear on it; these are appliquéd on to the ground fabric in gold and silver and coloured silks. The central scene is that of the crucifixion. On the left panel is shown Ralph Nevill, Fourth Earl of Westmoreland 1523; his seven sons kneel behind him. On the right panel is shown the earl's wife, Lady Catherine Strafford, and her thirteen daughters.

A large number of the mediaeval palls which are now the treasured possessions of the great city livery companies lack the refinement of *Opus Anglicanum* of the later period. A pall of the Saddlers' Company is made of red velvet embroidered with the arms of the company and the figures of angels. The Vintners' pall is of Italian velvet and cloth of gold and is embroidered with a representation of St Martin of Tours. Of special interest is the pall of the Fishmongers' Company. According to tradition, this magnificent mortuary cloth was used at the funeral of William Walworth in the reign of Richard II. The embroidery suggests that the pall is of later date, for it bears the united shields of the Stock-Fishmongers and the Salt-Fishmongers which were combined only in 1536 in the reign of Henry VIII. Supporting the united shields are the figures of a merman with armour of gold and a mermaid bearing a mirror in her hand.

The ground fabric is red-gold brocade of what is probably Flemish origin. The pall is rectangular, and on two short panels, worked in English embroidery, are shown figures of St Peter who was regarded as the patron saint of fishermen. He is also depicted on the centre panels, where he is shown receiving the keys of heaven from Christ.

The evidence relating to the date of this pall is of real importance in the study of English embroidery for it serves to extend the period of fine *Opus Anglicanum* by a term of more than one hundred and fifty years beyond that which is usually assigned to it.

It was probably inevitable that work of such fine quality as *Opus Anglicanum* should have its imitators. *Façon d'Angleterre* may have been a term referring to a spurious form of English embroidery. Charles the Bold, Duke of Burgundy, owned a magnificent cope of gold embroidery referred to as *façon d'Angleterre*. This appears to have been a term referring to work of acknowledged worth. St Henry, Emperor of Germany (973–1024), a connoisseur of fine embroideries, presented an embroidered cloth of *Opus Anglicanum* to the cathedral at Ratisbon. He also presented a rich embroidery to St Peter's at Rome. Whether work of this nature was made in England or by workers on the continent emulating the English embroiderers must henceforward remain a matter of conjecture.

The student of this period of embroidery is fortunate in the accessibility of specimens. Not only do the foremost museums yield rich stores but there are important embroideries in the provinces, at Salisbury, Cirencester, Ely, Carlisle and in churches at Chipping

Norton and Little Dean, Gloucestershire, East Langdon in Kent, and Lutterworth in Leicestershire.

The best work in *Opus Anglicanum* was done in the fourteenth century. During the fifteenth century, English embroidery lost its pre-eminence. Domestic and foreign troubles crowded on to the English scene in the later Middle Ages and these had drastic repercussions on all forms of art and craftsmanship. Culture, in all its aspects, received a severe setback from the ravages of the Black Death, the social and economic distress which affected all classes of society, the risings of the peasantry and the disorganized and fruitless attempts to obtain a speedy salve for all sores. Abroad, England was at strife (in the Hundred Years' War) with her near neighbour France. Moreover the country was becoming involved more and more in the general state of unrest that was engulfing Europe.

Embroidery work deteriorated. Stitchery was still complicated and precise and was still created on costly material but, compared to earlier work, it showed a decline. Much of the embroidery work was done on red and coloured velvet; this was not an innovation for some of the finest of the earlier work had been done on this ground. Appliqué work was much in favour. Embroidery work, as a whole, lacked the distinctiveness and creative power which were such strong characteristics of the earlier period.

The decline in embroidery did not occur precipitantly. The disbanding of the craft guilds and the dissolution of the monasteries had a dire effect. Interest became concentrated in more particular locations. The monastic workshops were the most productive centres and the courts of the nobility were in troubled times havens where much beautiful embroidery was made. The art of embroidery had, too, its economic worth. During the Wars of the Roses many noble ladies found in it a means of subsistence. Its psychological value must have been considerable also. The nobility resided, for the greater part, in castle fortresses, isolated as well as impregnable. The ladies within had but few out-of-door occupations; their ample leisure time was spent indoors. These circumstances reverberated to the advantage of the art of embroidery. During the Dark Ages the great ladies sewed on.

The Tudor period

The royal meeting at the Field of the Cloth of Gold was a spectacle emblematic of the magnificent pomp and display which characterized the European nations in the splendour of the Renaissance period. Italy and France set the standard and Henry VIII and England were not tardy in following their example. Close on five thousand men and women crossed the Channel to witness the royal spectacle in France and the richness of the English clothing on this occasion has passed into tradition. Records tell how nobles were ruined and their estates sold as a result of the national exhibition. It is significant too that a legend arose telling that a band of tailors in Henry's employ committed suicide, overcome with despair at their failure to meet the commissions allotted to them.

Equipment as well as clothing was taken over to France. These included highly decorated pavilions, tents, curtains and emblems. There were embroidered devices and standards including the red dragon, denoting the Welsh ancestry of the Tudor monarch, the arms of England, the symbols of Our Lady of the Trinity. According to the records of de Fleurenges, an able judge, the equipment of the English was less magnificent than that of France but, contrary to accepted expectations, it was the visitors who surpassed in the observance of the canons of good taste.

The traditions of good embroidery treasured in England had by this time weakened but they were by no means eclipsed. The religious houses prior to their suppression by Henry in 1536 were still influential centres of good taste and fine craftsmanship.

Costume and domestic requirements (plate 11) as well as ecclesiastical needs demanded the help of embroiderers. The many portraits of Henry VIII which have survived show that his clothes were elaborately embroidered. The royal example was followed closely by both men and women.

Catherine of Aragon, the unfortunate first wife of Henry, herself a skilled needle-woman, fostered the art of embroidery. When in retirement in Ampthill, Bedfordshire, she found solace in practising embroidery and taught it to her friends and protégées. She also taught the craft of lace-making. Her wardrobe lists refer to a number of embroidered articles and it is possible that her influence may have contributed to the so-called Spanish work or black work, a type of needlework which was to gather further popularity under her daughter, Queen Mary Tudor. In Spanish embroidery, the worker emphasized main outlines. When fillings were made, they were often introduced in red silk and in the form of diapering lines. When Spanish work was introduced on costume, gold thread in forms of scrolls and arabesques was added to the red and black work. It has also been suggested that the lavish use of black thread embroidery was occasioned by the influence of the newly-established printing presses. Many of the embroidery designs were close copies of those which were inspired by engravings and woodcuts.

A further development from mediaeval work was a type of embroidery called paned or paled work. The development of textiles is a fascinating story in itself and the interest in paned work reflects the extended range of fabrics now at the embroiderers' command. The worker produced effects now not only by variety of stitches and by blending and contrasting colours but by introducing fabrics of different texture and of different surface. An attractive hanging of especial charm in paned work is preserved in the Victoria and Albert Museum. The panels are in ivory damask and in crimson embroidered with gold. A trailing stem design is worked in brown silk cord. The hanging dates from the reign of the son of Henry VIII, the boy-king Edward VI.

Elizabeth's spectacular reign was a period of marked advance in every sphere of national life. There was an inevitable advance in British art and craftsmanship for the nation could draw inspiration from the whole of the newly-discovered world and from the spoils of many countries laid upon her shores. Powerful were the direct influences pouring on to her textiles from the East by way of the newly-formed trading companies. Contact with other nations, and the immigration of skilled workers from the Continent as a result of religious persecution, led to improved technical methods and forms of expression. Old native traditions were not engulfed in these. British craftsmanship recruited these forces to its own ends and its British character was never more pronounced than in the reign of the Great Elizabeth I.

There was a magnificent florescence of embroidery in the reign of Elizabeth. Good work had been done in the reigns of the previous Tudors. Nevertheless from the close of the fifteenth century to about 1575 there is a marked decadence following on previous work, although some authorities are prone to reserve judgement on the grounds that the dearth of specimens in that hiatus does not provide sufficient evidence. There is much proof to support the truth, however, that the Elizabethan period itself was characterized by a distinct and spectacular advance.

There was a powerful contributory factor in that the Elizabethan period produced embroideries of good craftsmanship worked not only by professional embroiderers, but also by an ever-increasing number of lay-people, who were growing enamoured of the gentler and more creative side of life. On a firm foundation of economic wealth, the middle classes of Britain were disciplining their overflowing vitality for the good of the nation. The housewife and the female society of Britain used their leisure time to embroider, not only on accustomed fabrics but on new fabrics and with the silk threads imported from the Levant. The technique they brought to bear on their work was more ambitious than that of the professional worker of the mediaeval period. During the reign of Queen Mary Tudor (1516–1558) steel needles had come into general use, replacing the wire ones which had hitherto been in vogue. Where the more professional workers were concerned, they received an impetus from the embroiderers' guilds which not only protected but developed their craft. Here England led the way and it is significant that European nations soon followed in the wake. In 1561 Elizabeth granted its first charter to the Broders' Company.

Elizabeth (1533–1603) was herself a skilled needlewoman though perhaps not with the ability of her half-sister, Mary, nor of her cousin, Mary Stuart. Expert opinion today is prone to question the fact that Elizabeth embroidered many of the specimens traditionally accredited as being her work. She had neither the time nor the ability for much fine work. Nevertheless, there exist records and specimens linked closely with her name. When a young girl, she was instructed in the art of needlework and worked diligently at her tasks. Her skill as an embroideress was not of a mean order. Her modest appeal to Henry IV of France requesting him to regard the scarf which she had embroidered for him with kindly eyes and to hide its defects under the wings of his good charity throws a new and more endearing light on a queen whom history tends to dub as arrogant. The New Year's Day Gift Rolls indicate Elizabeth's love of embroidery and the importance that was placed upon it in her time. In the year 1584, diplomats, powerful magnates and ecclesiasts presented the queen with dresses, mantles, petticoats, kirtles, slippers, all of which were magnificently embroidered after the fashion of the time. Lord Essex gave the queen a case for a doublet and a dress front of cut work decorated with silver spangles. Lord Walsingham presented her with an embroidered gown of light brown satin. Sir Philip Sydney's gifts during the queen's reign were numerous. On one occasion he gave her a pair of slippers on which were embroidered designs of seed pearls and garnets. Later he gave her a set of ruffs, decorated with spangles and a cambric chemise ornamented with 'Spanish' or black work. A tunic decorated after this manner, owned by Queen Elizabeth, is preserved in the Victoria and Albert Museum. The queen delighted in dresses, many of which were ornamented with designs in seed pearls and which were set with jewels. She is reputed to have possessed three thousand dresses at the time of her death. If this were so, it is likely that many of them were cut up in Stuart times so that the precious ornaments on them could be converted to other uses.

The nobility and the rising middle classes emulated the queen in their love of dress (plates 17 and 18). Men as well as women wore costumes which were richly embroidered. If the intervening centuries have been parsimonious in the wealth of specimens which they have bequeathed to us, art has come to the assistance of the modern student and the portraits of the Elizabethan period are both many and illuminating. Embroideries adorned the jackets and bodices of both men and women. Coifs, caps and gloves were similarly adorned.

The standard of daily comfort rose steadily throughout Tudor times. Greater privacy characterized the homes of all classes and the fortress castle was gradually abandoned for the delightful and graceful manor house. The nobility had no longer a monopoly of the luxuries of life; the strong and virile middle class demanded much from life and contributed much towards it. Referring to the new order that had arisen in Britain, William Harrison writing his *Chronicles of England* in 1577, says:

> In the houses of knights and gentlemen, merchantmen and some other wealthy citizens, it is not so *geson* [rare] to behold generally their great provision of tapestry, Turkey work... and fine linen. Many farmers garnish... their beds with tapestry and fine silk hangings and their tables with carpets and napery... whereby the wealth of the country... doth infinitely appear.

Table and floor carpets were embroidered and wall hangings contributed not only to greater privacy within the homes but to their aesthetic pleasure as well. Beds were objects of great splendour. They were of large dimensions, a traditional size for royal beds being eleven feet square. Such beds were placed in a living or state room. The space between the wall and the bed was used as a reception room at the time of the monarch's levée or uprising. Even when greater privacy in personal life was stressed, the gigantic beds were preserved in the great manor houses, monasteries and hostelries for transport facilities were as yet inadequate and necessitated ample accommodation at night for travellers.

The invention of printing had brought about a complete revolution in the production of books. Embroidered bindings enhanced such books in Tudor and Stuart times. It was as though these individual ornamentations satisfied a need in the lives of people hitherto unconvinced as to the worth of mass production. The writing of books had erstwhile been a matter of detailed care and embellishment. Now that the printing press evolved the text, the bindings became fields for the embroiderer's art.

Fortunately, many examples of these embroidered books have come down to us and may be seen to-day in the British Museum, the Victoria and Albert Museum and in the library of the British and Foreign Bible Society.

The embroidered binding was not entirely an innovation. A 'forel' or loose cover, finely embroidered, had been used in mediaeval times to carry books or manuscripts but with the advent of the printed book, new ground was exposed. Originality was a strong characteristic of the embroidered covers. Many of the designs were elaborate, bearing borders featuring arabesques of gold, crests studded with precious stones and jewelled clasps.

Interlacings of gold and silver threads are to be seen on an embroidered book preserved in the Bodleian Museum, Oxford. The cover and text are said to be the work of Queen Elizabeth (plate 10). The book is dedicated to Katherine Parr, the last of Henry's queens and her initials and symbol, the pansy, are worked upon it. Elizabeth is said to have translated the manuscript from the French in the year 1544, when she was residing at Ashridge. The book bears the title *Mirroir or Glasse of the Synneful Soul*. Another book in the same museum has a more usual covering of black velvet. It is *The Epistles of St Paul* printed in London in 1578. In gold and silver thread there are inscribed on the cover exhortations to study the scriptures. Within is a note written by Elizabeth.

> I walke manie times into the pleasant fields of the Holy Scriptures... that having tasted of their sweetness I may the less perceive the bitterness of this miserable life.

Elizabeth is accredited with having embroidered the beautiful covering of a bible printed in London in 1583 by Christopher Barker. If this is so, it is probable that she was assisted by one of her ladies-in-waiting who must have been a skilled needlewoman. The Tudor rose plays an important part in the design which is displayed on a groundwork of crimson velvet. The embroidery is in coloured silks and gold and silver thread and seed pearls.

Velvet did not lend itself readily to stitchery ornament. The Elizabethan embroiderers therefore resorted to the use of appliqué. Motifs were cut out in linen, silk or other material, these were embroidered and were then applied to a groundwork of velvet. The final effect was pleasing and sumptuous and the worker had the satisfaction of having created a covering or costume which rivalled closely the rich brocades that were now being manufactured.

This ingenious method of decoration was used widely on ecclesiastical vestments. Its resources were realized too in upholstery. Wall hangings of the Tudor period preserved at Hardwick Hall had a groundwork of black velvet with appliqué designs in silk. The designs are ambitious and pictorial. On one, figures are grouped under Gothic arches and on another is depicted the figure of a woman holding in her hand a book entitled *Faith*. At Penshurst, the upholstery of Queen Elizabeth's room is in appliqué. Originally, the room contained in the accustomed manner, wall hangings in similar fabrics and designs.

Mary, Queen of Scots (1542–87), was diligent in her pursuit of needlework during her long years of captivity. She had been instructed in her girlhood in the French court under the supervision of her mother-in-law, Catherine de'Medici, herself an able needlewoman. Mary's interest in needlework was such that she founded a school of embroidery at Châteaudun before she embarked for Scotland.

Contemporary accounts of the queen's devotion to needlework are numerous and there are also many accounts describing the nature of her work. Of particular interest is a letter from Drummond of Hawthornden to Ben Jonson, dated 1st July 1619, wherein he describes some of Mary's embroidery – emblems and mottoes worked in coloured silk and gold thread for furnishings of a bed of state. He refers to an anagram on the queen's name, Marie Stuart – *Sa virtu m'attire* – with loadstone having reference to the crucifix before which the queen kneels. The emblem of Mary's mother, Mary of Lorraine, showed a phoenix and above the flames was the inscription *En ma fin git mon commencement*. The emblem of Henry II was a crescent; that of Francis I, a salamander. A design showing three birds pierced with an eagle stood for Godfrey of Boulogne. As her own emblem and that of her son, the young prince James, Mary embroidered a ship with a broken mast. There were also embroidered many other devices and mottoes, including the arms of Scotland, France and England.

Various embroideries attributed to Mary, Queen of Scots have been preserved in those castles where she spent her captivity (plates 12 and 13). Embroidered work consisting of curtains and furnishing cloths preserved at Oxburgh Hall, Norfolk, show the vogue for heraldic emblems and appliqué work with the motifs embroidered in gold thread.

The floral tradition of embroidery became more pronounced in the Tudor period. In the Middle Ages floral borders, prominent on the margins of illuminated manuscripts, had been introduced. Many of the flowers were geometric in form. In the Renaissance era it was usual to portray flowers in their natural colours. The total effect of the floral arrangements might be formal but the flower motifs were portrayed naturally. As the sixteenth century advanced, the floral sprays attained a greater flexibility and movement without detracting from their charming simplicity. The designs show that they were inspired by the common flowers of field and garden. On the Tudor embroideries, one sees those flowers which are referred to so frequently by Shakespeare, Spenser, Donne and others of the Elizabethan poets. The strawberry fruit, together with its broad leaves and trailing stems, was introduced into main designs. It was the *wild* strawberry which was embroidered; the fruit was a familiar delicacy and was cried around the streets of London to the tune of fourpence a bushel.

The general interest in the flowers and fruits of the English countryside was probably greater in Tudor times than in the succeeding centuries. In 1597 appeared Gerard's *Herbal*; the woodcuts in this book were consulted freely by needleworkers of the close of Elizabeth's reign and the Stuart period. The clear-cut lines of the designs, which showed no elaborate details, made these woodcuts eminently suitable for reproduction in embroidery. Earlier herbals too were illustrated with similar woodcuts. The work of the Swiss naturalist, Von Gesner, entitled *Catalogues Plantarum* and the more general work *Historia Animalum* yielded illustrations of plants, animals, birds and fishes. These too were provided by a work already well-known in mediaeval ages, the *Physiologus*, though the legendary symbols were now at a discount. Pattern books were also introduced into England from Italy and from Germany.

The founding of the East India Company in 1599 had far-reaching effects on embroidery, affecting materials and design.

Stuart embroideries

The Stuart dynasty, established at the beginning of the seventeenth century, was to be subject to overwhelming changes during the period of its existence. Twice it was overturned and in its course it was directed by widely differing monarchs. Moreover it was interrupted by the austere and puritanical interregnum under the stern rule of Cromwell.

Art and craftmanship in this period were inevitably influenced by national vicissitudes. Embroidery, among other things, underwent far-reaching changes. For a time, the style characteristic of Elizabethan embroidery continued. Spanish work was favoured, its designs receiving an impetus from the advanced and ornate work displayed in engraved armour (plate 18). Appliqué work was also in great vogue and this expanded into the 'stump' work (plate 22) which became so marked a feature of the embroidered pictures of the Stuart period. Following on the Restoration, the style known as *chinoiserie* experienced a vogue. This, in turn, yielded to the more harmonious influences emanating from France and from Holland, resulting from close political association between Britain and those countries.

Portraits of the time of the early Stuarts indicate that the costumes of both men and women continued to be embroidered elaborately in polychrome silks long after the death of Elizabeth. Floral embroidery long held sway and Spanish work was much in demand. The many fine specimens that have survived bear evidence of skill and of precision in workmanship. Designs were frequently based on scroll patterns and many of these bore motifs of birds and flowers, worked in petit point and appliquéd on to the fabric. The outlines of black work were usually in back stitching or chain work which provided a solid edge. Relief was sometimes introduced on 'solid' motifs such as those of birds or fruit. At times, gold and silver thread (plate 20) were couched alongside the scroll lines and this was what was known as 'Spanish stitch' according to the evidence of old inventories. The name was derived from the fact that Catherine of Aragon was accredited with having introduced it. Spanish or black embroidery was used on jackets (plates 20 and 23), surcoats, coats and caps (both of men and of women), wall hangings, bed furnishings and book covers. Many specimens of this type of embroidery are housed in the Victoria and and Albert Museum.

Much of the popularity of Spanish work rested on the fact that it was particularly acceptable to those who sought a quieter taste in dress and who eschewed the brighter colours and more elaborate accessories characteristic of the Cavalier period. Black work looked well on satin and in simple trailing designs. It is featured on the well-known portrait of Mary Sidney, Countess of Pembroke, which is in the National Portrait Gallery, London. The fashion for black work continued until late in the eighteenth century.

'Yellow silk' embroidery was in a sense a development of black work. In this, tiny padded panels embroidered with heraldic devices were embroidered in yellow silk on ivory satin. When the panels were assembled, the whole assumed a rich and unusual quilted effect.

Designs for embroidery in general were still inspired by the old herbals. Many were obtained from samplers which were now worked so ornately and so universally. These samplers, meant at first to be vehicles of design, came during the Stuart period to have artistic worth in themselves. Embroiderers were content to concentrate their efforts in the creation of a sampler, the working of which might occupy the greater part of their leisure time. The development and characteristic features of these samplers afford an intriguing study as they were worked in most European countries. They provided, too, a richer and more personal source of design than the more stereotyped and more frugal pattern books of this and of succeeding centuries.

Among the more general books providing illustrations for embroidery were the *Insectorum* of Thomas Moufet, which was first published in 1607 and the published illustrations of Peter Stent issued between 1640 and 1662. These provided designs of birds, beasts, flowers, emblems and personages. Quarles' book on *Emblems* and Simpson's book of *Flowers, Fruits, Birds and Beasts* provided further guidance in illustrations.

Of a more directly technical nature was the famous book *The Schole House of the Needle* by Richard Shoreleyker which was first published in 1624. The title page of a later edition of this book carries the explanatory caption:

'Here followeth certain patternes of cut workes and but once printed before. Also sundry sort of spots as Flowers, Birds, Fishes etc. and will fitly serve to be wrought, some with Gould, some with Silke and one with Crewell or otherwise at your pleasure.'

Another popular book was that of John Taylor, known as the Water Poet. The title of the 1640 edition was inscribed *The Needles Excellency: A new book wherein are divers admirable works wrought with the needle for the pleasure and profit of the industrious.*

Embroidered pictures were much favoured in the Stuart period (plate 22). An examination of these indicates that they were the result of long, patient and laborious effort. Kendrick in his authoritative work *English Needlework* writes:

> There is no European country in which more time and skill have been expended than in England over the working of panels for mounting as pictures or for hanging as bed valances and the like. Perhaps it was the lack in England of a flourishing school of portrait and landscape painting, such as that of Holland, for example, which gave the needleworkers their opportunity.

The embroidered pictures bore a close resemblance to the tapestries of the time and were undoubtedly inspired by them. Many were worked in petit point in silk thread over canvas. Petit point stitch was a greater favourite than cross stitch which had been in use in Tudor days. But many other stitches were used in addition for the fanciful designs of the pictures called into use a wide range and many new stitches were created. John Taylor catalogued a number of these stitches in the doggerel:

> For tent worke, raised worke, first worke, laid worke, net worke,
> Most curious purl or rare Italian cut worke,
> Fire, ferne stitch, finny stitch, new stitch, chain stitch,
> Brave bred stitch, fisher stitch, Irish stitch and Queen stitch,
> The Spanish stitch, Rosemary stitch and mowle stitch,
> The smarting whip stitch, back stitch and cross stitch;
> All these are good, and this we must allow,
> And they are everywhere in practice now.

The subjects of these pictures were equally varied. They were a hotch-potch of anachronisms. Classical and mythological scenes were set against Renaissance architecture. Biblical characters were dressed in the height of Stuart fashion. Pastoral settings were given to court scenes and borders of mythical animals bounded the whole. Animals, birds and insects had by now assumed a new symbolism: the Tudor rose signified the union of the Houses of Lancaster and of York, the unicorn was the device of James I, the stag and the strawberry were heraldic emblems of the Clan Frazer of Scotland (the stag was also the device of Richard II), the lion and the leopard stood for England, the broom pod for the Plantagenets. Special badges of Charles I were embroidered with caterpillars and butterflies. Charles II's escape in an oak tree was commemorated in oak tree and acorn designs – all these symbols figured prominently in Stuart pictures.

Portraits were favourite themes for needle paintings. Of particular interest are the many pictures of Charles I which have survived (plate 21). It is possible that many of them were worked by fervent loyalists as expressions of their beliefs and also as mementoes of the royal martyrdom. Many of the portraits were copied from portraits of Charles made by Anthony Van Dyck and other artists of the time. Skill of a high degree went into the making of a portrait now preserved in the Victoria and Albert Museum – strands of the king's hair have been worked in among the silk threads. In general the portrait embroideries were much influenced by the contemporary miniaturists. Embroiderers inscribed their work much as the miniaturists did though their mottoes appeared on the fabric instead of on the frame.

Stump work (plate 19), which was so characteristic a feature of Stuart pictures, is believed to have had its origin in Italy. The stump work of Italy was, however, superior to that of Britain and particularly so in the observance of the rules of proportion and perspective. Raised and padded effects were already recognized in the English tradition of embroidery. It had had its place in Elizabethan embroidery, much of it representing children's work.

Biblical themes were popular. At the Lady Lever Art Gallery in Port Sunlight is a realistic picture of Pharaoh and the Egyptian army being drowned in the Red Sea. The Victoria and Albert Museum has a stump work picture showing *The Finding of Moses*; the child prophet is designed as the infant Duke of York.

In the reign of Charles I, the king and queen were the most popular subjects for embroidery. It was claimed that pieces of their clothing were introduced into the representations of their majesties. Sometimes the royal couple were embroidered in a disguised form. A picture in the Victoria and Albert Museum entitled *King Solomon receiving the Queen of Sheba* is ostensibly representative of King Charles I and Queen Henrietta Maria. The canopy is worked in relief in coloured silks and gold thread, the latter always proving a difficult medium wherein to work. Brocade curtains are embroidered in gold thread. The king and queen are shown dressed magnificently, wearing crowns of gold thread set with pearls; natural hair has been introduced. The faces are of silk and of wool, with black thread indicating the features. Some of the robes are in appliqué work embroidered in loose stitches. The queen's dress of gold brocade has been enhanced with embroidery in gold and silver thread. Around her neck are real pearls and real lace trims her dress. Symbolic devices relating to the period, such as the oak tree with stump work acorns, are much in evidence.

Humour and charm characterize these pictures which, full of anachronisms as they are, are of special documentary evidence to the social historian of the Stuart period.

The interest in relief work in embroidery may have been occasioned in part by the nature of the objects on which it was used. Embroidery of this kind was used to ornament Stuart caskets, trays and mirrors and the needleworker sought to emulate the craftsman in inlaid work and carving.

Stuart caskets (plate 19), often fitted with secret drawers and recesses, were covered with satin and with velvet and were embroidered in formal patterns in long stitches. Central medallions were very popular and these were coloured in tones to harmonize with the gold and silver fittings on the corners and locks of the boxes. Kendrick gives an illuminating account of the part children played in the embroidering of these caskets. A charming casket now preserved in the Whitworth Art Gallery in Manchester is the work of a certain Hannah Smith. It represents two years' labour undertaken at the age of twelve. Her own account of the making has been preserved along with the casket.

The yere of our Lord being 1657.
    If ever I have any thoughts about the time I went to Oxford as it may be I may, when I have forgotten the time, to satisfie myself I may loock in this paper and find it;
    I went to Oxford in the yere of 1654 and my being thare near 2 yere, for I went in 1654 and I stayed there 1655 and I cam away in 1656; and I was allmost 12 years. of age when I went, and I mad an end of my cabbinete at Oxford and my quenes... and my cabbinet was mad up in the yere of 1656 at London. I have ritten this to satisfi myself and thos that shall inquir about it Hannah Smith.

Many such cabinets were worked in the time of the Commonwealth, a period far more sympathetic to the arts than past verdicts would indicate.

Small trays and trinket boxes were similarly decorated with stump work embroidery and mirrors were lavishly embroidered in this manner. Here the needleworker encroached on the cabinet maker's domain. The glass was small, for it was expensive, but it was fitted with a wide frame. This usually carried four panels of embroidery, punctuated at the corners with symbolic designs of fruits and flowers and animals such as the usual lion, leopard, unicorn and stag. Scriptural scenes adorned the panel at times; royal portraits were, however, more popular.

Beadwork was introduced into a number of embroidered pictures and in certain instances superseded stitchery entirely. A certain hardness and lack of flexibility characterized scenes in beadwork and needleworkers reverted to the use of threads.

Embroidered book-binding continued in favour until the close of the reign of Charles II. Definite advance had by this time been made in the realm of leather and cloth binding and the printing press had become more versatile. Where a personal touch was required, embroidered bookbindings were introduced. They were now smaller, almost diminutive in size and were decorated with many motifs, heraldic, pictorial and floral. Petit point was a favourite stitch on canvas grounds; on silk, satin and velvet the more usual stitches were chain and split stitches. Sometimes a net of gold or silver thread was made and this was couched on to the cover. Seed pearls were used as an ornamentation as were also motifs cut out in metal. Some of the most renowned of these embroidered covers were worked by the nuns of Little Gidding in the first half of the seventeenth century. Covers are in green and in purple velvet and there are scatterings, chiefly of crowns, in gold; these books are now in the British Museum. There are also very many other specimens of embroidered books of this period such as the attractive copy of Bacon's *Essays* in the Bodleian Library, ornamented with a portrait of the Duke of Buckingham surrounded by a design in gold foliage.

Dutch and French influences penetrated into Britain under William and Mary and also under Anne. This was an important period in architecture and remarkable advances were made in interior decoration. Wren and Vanbrugh dominated in the realm of architecture; Kneller was the doyen of portrait painters. The Franco-Italian style of decorative painting prevailed, a characteristic example of this being the mural decorations made by Verrio on the grand staircase at Hampton Court. This palace and Kensington Palace were furnished in the baroque style which dominated the furniture and costume of the period. Curtains and wall hangings in bold designs and in muted shades of blues and greens, pinks and yellows characterized what came to be known as Jacobean work. These served as happy models for furnishing fabrics of a later age.

The eighteenth century

Eastern influences grew more prevalent in embroidery as the eighteenth century advanced. The needleworkers were reaping the full harvest of forces which had been flowing since the reign of Elizabeth when commercial companies trading with the Near East were established. But now the influence of the Far East was making itself felt directly. Oriental influence was not altogether new in Europe for wares from India and

China had been distributed in Europe by way of the mediaeval fairs. Turkey work, resembling carpet work, was practised in Europe in Tudor days; motifs featuring in European embroidery were worked after the manner of this oriental technique. In the latter half of the seventeenth century, far eastern influences engulfed western Europe. The strength of this great tide cannot be measured adequately by the modern student accustomed to the tradition of things eastern in western life. Even as the flood of Renaissance art had flowed over the Gothic tradition, so now did the tide of eastern culture engulf the revival of classical antiquity.

The influence of both Chinese and Indian art was felt especially in textiles (plate 27). Circumstances contributing to this impact included the opening up of far eastern waters to British sailors and the rapid increase in trade with the East. Materials, including rich fabrics, were brought to Britain and were bought immediately. Fabrics of more native texture and design fell into disrepute. Consequently, workshops and individuals hastened to copy the bright and even florid colours of eastern fabrics with their attractive and bizarre designs. Thus arose the vogue for *chinoiserie* as it was termed in England; the French term for this particular style being *rachinage*. Chinese designs appeared not only on upholstery and wall hangings but also on costumes.

Bandar in British India was the main clearing house for the decorative linens, cottons and chintzes of the East. Embroiderers in England forsook the velvets and brocades and used linen (plate 26) as a foundation fabric for their work. They called into use a special material made with a linen warp and cotton weft. This was strong enough to carry the heavy embroidery motifs, worked no longer in polychrome silks but in coloured worsteds. When advances were made in the construction of spinning machines and when these were capable of manufacturing strong cotton thread of sufficient force to carry the strain of the loom on the warp, the embroiderers reverted to a fabric made entirely of cotton.

A fresh impulse was given to trade with the East when William III established a new East India Company. The rococo style prevalent in France owed much of its inspiration to China and, as often in the realm of things artistic, England followed the example of France. This period of baroque yielded at first designs which were odd and irregular but as the eighteenth century progressed it became evident that a discriminating taste was forming. Designs on embroideries often featured Chinese or other oriental landscapes. The colours were inspired by the furniture and lacquer work of the East and showed prevailing tones of black and of brown and subdued shades of blue, of green and of yellow (plate 31). Landscape scenes were used in particular for the upholstering of settees, daybeds, chairs, stools and screens. Costumes and wall hangings were decorated with floral designs. Many species of plants were shown on a single thick and trailing stem. Eastern motifs, including the ever-popular chrysanthemum, were displayed. Birds were favourite units in a design and were represented with bright plumage. Eastern temples, pagodas and landscapes were introduced as fitting backgrounds.

When the needleworkers recognized the capabilities and limits of their medium, results were pleasing (plate 28). At times, however, too pronounced efforts were made to make the embroidery resemble a painting and the stitches were varied to resemble the effects produced by the brush. Thus the intrinsic characteristics of the stitches themselves were placed at a discount and the tendency was to draw attention away from the beauty of form, the texture and ingenuity of the needlework.

Much of the degeneracy of embroidery in the eighteenth and the succeeding centuries was occasioned by the development of fine fabrics and rich brocades (plate 27). Considering the advance made in this realm, it is somewhat surprising that such an immeasurable amount of time and of dexterity was spent in the ornamenting of fabrics for upholstery. There was a tradition of such work, it is true. Needlework for upholstery was not an innovation. Indeed even in the Middle Ages there had evolved a special form of needlework to meet this need, the *Opus Pluvarium* or cushion work. Upholstery was detached from the wooden chair and benches in the earlier ages. Cushions wore out quickly; hence the frequent references to them in inventories. It is interesting to consider how magnificent copes and other vestments were converted into cushions and similar articles.

The advance made in the styles of furniture during the eighteenth century provided the needleworker with greater scope (plate 31). Upholstered furniture was now the rule and the finer suites were provided with coverings of tapestry or of embroidery. Floral patterns were much in favour. Motifs were treated naturalistically. Baskets of flowers were usual designs, their popularity being ensured by the publication of a set of engraved patterns. Oriental touches characterized many floral designs, appearing in the form of oriental figures or borders with eastern flowers and leaves. Western designs reasserted themselves on the fabrics used for upholstery and as in tapestry, workers created scenes from biblical and classical history, and from mythology. A chair with embroidered covering in the Victoria and Albert Museum displays scenes from Virgil's *Æneid*.

Pole screens are characteristic mementoes from the eighteenth century. They had a utilitarian value serving as a protection from heat or draught. Some took the form of hand screens and were mounted artistically in wood or ivory. As vehicles for embroidery, they provided an entrancing field for the needleworker for they offered many of the qualities of a needlework picture, being spared the friction to which an upholstered seat or chair back was subject. On these flat panels, rectangular, oval or polygonal, floral and pastoral scenes were portrayed.

Embroidered pictures retained their popularity in the eighteenth century. Here again, pastoral scenes were favoured. Paintings and engravings of the time were sources of inspiration. In 1734 appeared Robert Furber's book *The Flower Garden* providing as many as four hundred designs. A little later a similar book was issued by Heckell. By now too there were a number of ladies' magazines in circulation providing suggestions and designs for embroidery.

The interest in samplers which characterized each succeeding generation was not only maintained in the eighteenth century but it was intensified. Elaborate inscriptions, quaint pictures and ambitious map samplers were worked showing that this particular expression of needlework had advanced far from its original purpose of being an 'example' or sample of stitchery.

Embroidery had to a remarkable extent maintained its character of individuality until well into the eighteenth century (plates 26, 28, 29). Many designs from this time on, however, were mass-produced and some needlework designs were bought ready for embroidering. Landscapes and the faces and hands of figures were painted in readiness. It has been suggested that this represented the work of the lesser artists of the great period of English portrait painting. The style of dress favoured by figures such as those which Sir Joshua Reynolds painted looked charming in the needlework pictures. The high-waisted bodices of lawn and muslin and flowing robes fashionable in the Georgian periods looked well in embroidery representations.

Fine, neat stitchery with an almost total neglect of shading characterized these needle-work pictures. The work was done in fine floss silk or crewel wools; sometimes a little chenille or metallic thread was introduced for glistening effects. Appliqué panels in chiffon with shaded stitchery were occasionally attached to figures. Reminiscent of memorials were the needlework pictures worked on white silk; here the stitchery was in black silk and hair and designs often took the form of portraits.

The Victorian period and after

Until comparatively recently, it has been axiomatic to decry the taste in needlework of the Victorian era. It may be that, even as yet, we are too near to the nineteenth century to see Victorian forms of expression in their true perspective.

At the same time, it is difficult to set up a defence for much of the embroidered work that was created in that epoch. The degeneracy already apparent in English needlecraft in the eighteenth century was accelerated in the following century when embroiderers displayed a great delight in wool crewel work.

There was a distinct revival of interest in coloured embroideries (sometimes known as Berlin work) worked in wool and sometimes in silk. Designs were heterogeneous, em-bracing biblical and pastoral scenes and curious representations of plant and animal life. There was also an increased interest in print work, which was a close imitation of stippled engravings, worked on a ground of white silk in thread of black, brown or grey. As canvas was used for most grounds, cross stitch retained its popularity. Almost every child was initiated into embroidery work through sampler work.

In the latter half of the eighteenth century and the first half of the nineteenth, there was a universal vogue for Miss Linwood's *Pictures in Worsted*. The scenes comprised sixty-four designs and they aimed at copying in wool work famous oil paintings. Miss Linwood's own embroideries were esteemed as works of art. In 1798 she held an exhibi-tion of her work in London. She was offered the sum of £3,000 for her embroidered wall hanging *Salvator Mundi* but she refused the sum and bequeathed the needlework picture to Queen Victoria. Other of her pictures include the portrait of Napoleon which she worked at the age of seventy and which is among the properties of the Victoria and Albert. More spectacular is her picture *The Judgement of Cain* which took ten years to complete. Models similar to those of Miss Linwood were evolved by Mrs Delaney and Miss Knowles and these enjoyed a similar popularity and were worked assiduously. Throughout the nineteenth century, women of all classes worked cross stitch pictures on canvas. The colours they used were crude; deep crimson, rich purple, royal blue, vivid magenta and emerald green were mixed indiscriminately. Berlin wool was also used to portray scenes such as were inspired by Landseer's paintings, incidents in the life of Christ and stirring events in national history. Wool embroidery of this nature was not confined to pictures. It was used to embellish sofas, footstools, screens and other articles of furniture.

The embroidered work of the Victorians must be considered against its historical setting before judgement is passed on it (plates 32, 35–37). This was a period when inventions and innovations crowded in upon each other and rapid advance was being made in all forms of textile crafts. The embroiderers of the Victorian age *did* keep alive the spirit of handicraft in a machine age and the technical excellence of their embroidery, if not their taste in design and colour harmonies, must be acclaimed.

Nor must the Victorian Age be regarded as a period of total darkness even in the matter of design and colour. Valiant souls such as William Morris warred in the crusade demanding a return to the spirit of mediaeval craftsmanship. He turned his attention not only to design but to the materials used in the creation of embroideries: he battled against the scientific advance of his times and decried the use of embroidered silks which had been coloured by coal tar or aniline dyes, the discovery of which had been made in 1858. He also foresaw the divorce that was bound to come between true handicraft and machine-made goods.

Writing in 1893 in his *Arts and Crafts Essays* 'On Dyeing as an Art', he commented on the subject of aniline dyes.

> Of these dyes it must be enough to say that their discovery, whilst conferring the greatest honour on the abstract science of chemistry, and while doing great service to capitalists in their hunt after profits, has terribly injured the art of dyeing, and for the general public has nearly destroyed it as an art. Henceforward, there is an absolute divorce between the commercial process and the art of dyeing. Anyone wanting to produce dyed textiles with any artistic quality in them must entirely forego the modern and commercial methods in favour of those which are as old as Pliny, who speaks of them as being old in his time.

It was due to William Morris, Sir Edward Burne-Jones and his school of artists that embroidery was infused with new and healthy life. Interested in interior decoration, they allotted to embroidery its legitimate place and prepared designs which occupied women over long periods of time but which fully justified the expenditure of time and effort when completed. Many of the designs prepared by the artists had a close affinity with the cartoons which they prepared for the tapestry work which they sponsored so assiduously. An unfinished needlework picture in the Victoria and Albert Museum gives real insight into the type of work done at this time. It is a representation of Sir Edward Burne-Jones' *Star of Bethlehem*. The figures portrayed are those of the Virgin and Child, the Angel and the Wise Men in the setting of the stable. The colours are harmonious and shading is introduced into the garments. Flesh is worked in solid shading in very fine silk and an effect of stippling is achieved in the groundwork which is covered over with stitchery.

Far-reaching also has been the influence of the Royal School of Needlework which had its beginnings in an establishment founded in London in 1872. Conscious of the execrable taste of the time, the directors of this school fostered at first an imitation of seventeenth-century work and then progressed to the teaching of sound design and the practice of embroidery. It reflects on the intelligence of the populace that both in England and in America embroiderers responded quickly and acknowledged the canons of good taste. Similar schools were set up under royal patronage in many of the European countries. America gave gracious recognition to the worth of English work and when the Society of Decorative Art became established in the United States, English designs and practices were followed under the tuition of English teachers.

Advance in the craft of embroidery was cut short by World War 1. Following on the armistice, the value of embroidery work as a form of occupational therapy was recognized in convalescent hospitals. Men became once more interested in embroidery and although as a masculine craft it is still subservient to the feminine, its practice has continued to increase and has been accelerated following on the tragedies of World War II. The stress of modern life has also resulted in the practice of embroidery as a form of recreation by expression in design and colour.

The two World Wars brought a succession of refugees into Britain and new techniques and design were introduced into the work done in this country. Designs of the twentieth century are influenced considerably by the various schools of painting and design. The expressions are sometimes straightforward, sometimes confused but all have the asset of being virile and progressive. The embroiderer of today is no slavish copyist and the portents for the future are reasonably sound.

5 *France*

The barbarity of western Europe was intensified by the overthrow of the Roman Empire in the fifth century. The monarchies which arose were preoccupied with war. Trade and commerce, manufactures, arts and crafts fell into abeyance. Indeed, it is suprising that they were preserved in any measure in the centuries of total darkness which then engulfed western Europe. The influence of Christianity prevailed, however, in certain cases. The French historian Mignet in his *Historical Studies* emphasizes this truth when he declares that 'monasteries were the workshops in which the traditions of ancient arts were maintained and perpetuated.'

It is not surprising, therefore, that many of the early embroidered cloths of France were made for the use of the church; and vestments, hangings and funeral palls were usually ornamented with biblical scenes. The animals portrayed had a symbolic value and the beginnings of heraldry soon became evident. The royal bee as worked in a design bearing three hundred of these motifs shown on the funeral pall of King Childeric and also the lion on the numerous cloths known as *leonata* show the development of this branch of embroidery. Another emblem in growing evidence was the cross, which was usually set in a circle. Cloths bearing this motifs were referred to as *stauros* from the Greek word meaning a cross. During the fourth and fifth centuries, the cross either plain or in a looped form taken from the Egyptian hieroglyphics and often set with jewels, became a recognized symbol of Christianity and this, together with the letters Alpha and Omega, acquired an established place in embroidery.

Most of the embroidery was worked on linen in worsted or silk thread. Some gold was introduced into the work but it was not used lavishly and where it did appear it was usually couched. Other stitches were comparatively simple and included stem, satin and feather stitch.

Charlemagne (768–814) did much by his strong and enlightened rule to extend civilization and develop the arts among his people. Commerce and manufactures flourished in his reign and he fostered industries in Flanders, Brabant and other regions and maintained a high standard of culture at his court. It is recorded that his mother, Bertha (nicknamed 'of the Big Feet') taught the art of embroidery to Charlemagne's daughters while the emperor's aunt, St Giselle, fostered skill in needlework in the many convents which she established in Aquitaine and Provence.

Valuable information concerning the life of Charlemagne and the manners and customs of his times have been bequeathed to us in the writings of a monk, Eginhard, who lived at St Gall in the time of the great emperor. In the *Vita Karolis Imperatoris* one may learn of Charlemagne's state dress comprising 'a close-fitting vest or jacket of gold embroidery, sandals or slippers set with precious stones; also a cloak or mantle fastened by a golden brooch or fibula and a crown of gold, glistening with gems'.

Largely as the result of direct contact with the East in the time of the crusades, materials or textiles became richer and more varied during the Middle Ages. Embroiderers in western Europe became familiar with cloths bearing names such as samit, cendal, cloth of gold, velvet, camoca, silver bandekin and many others. These new weavings provide a subject of study in themselves and an able survey of them appears in Francisque Michel's work *Etoffes de Soie*.

Greater variety of materials resulted in a greater variety of designs; which continued to be as straightforward as before, although oriental and Byzantine motifs were adopted early. Embroiderers were attracted by heraldic subjects and biblical scenes, particularly those of a militant nature, were also portrayed. As the Middle Ages progressed, it became evident that deliberate efforts were being made to perfect and refine the technique of embroidery. This was achieved but only by sacrificing much of the attractive boldness and purity of style which had characterized earlier work.

It was usual for kings and nobles to present churches with a proportion of the spoils taken in the crusading campaigns. Similarly, new embroideries were made for this purpose. Hangings for the walls of churches and for altars were ornamented with coloured silks and often bore figures representing the patron saint of the church to which they were dedicated. Heraldic bearings tended to appear in the borders of these cloths and also on ecclesiastical garments.

This was a period when heraldic crests were created and stabilized. The right of wearing a coat of arms was granted to a noble family by the king. The heraldic crest in its appropriate colours was displayed in knightly tournaments in days of peace and on banners and pennons in time of war. During the twelfth century, the *fleurs-de-lys* became established as royal insignia. Under Louis the Young, the motifs were prolific and took the form of powderings on tabards and banners but under Charles v, however, the *fleurs* were reduced to three, each bloom symbolizing a person of the Holy Trinity.

The heraldic embroideries of France are in themselves an attractive study both with regard to the intricacies of the designs and on account of their potentialities, calling into being an advanced technique and a wide range of new stitches.

A higher standard of domestic and personal comfort was developing with the advance of the Middle Ages. Textile materials including silks, velvets, damasks and satins were introduced into homes to adorn articles of personal wear and use. With regard to this there is the most illuminating *Book of Crafts* written by Etienne Boileau of Paris who held the important office of provost of the Merchant Gilds during the decade 1258–1268. The references are wide but among them appear some which have a direct relationship to textiles and their ornamentation. (See page 17.)

An early French inventory refers to Margaret the emblazoner, who ornamented pouches with coats of arms. These pouches were essential accessories to the garb of the early Middle Ages. They were hung on girdles and although serving much the same purpose as purses today, they were also used for carrying prayer books and sacred relics.

Many specimens of these pouches have survived and the treasuries of many of the French cathedrals are rich in the possession of them. A large number of the designs shown on them were suggested by those that appeared in the illuminated manuscripts of the thirteenth century. Scenes depicted were varied but a constant theme was that characteristic of the thought of the time – the fall of man and the emphasis on his animal nature. During the fourteenth century and in less militant times, designers were influenced by the current romantic movement and expressed themselves through the media of motifs linked with literary epics such as *The Romance of the Rose*.

In the creation of these embroidered pouches, France gained an international reputation and the chief centre of manufacture was to be found at Caen in northern France. The pouches were called *tasques*, a name derived from the Italian word *tasca* meaning a purse. There appears to have been a solid foundation to the eulogy on Caen purses made by Charles Bourgueville, Sieur de Bras, in 1588 when he expressed in his *Récherches et Antiquités sur la ville de Caen* that 'none made in other towns can compare with them for choiceness, character and exquisite materials, such as velvet of all colours, gold, silver and other threads or in suitability for the use of nobles, justices, ladies and maidens so that it is a common proverb to speak of "Caen purses above all others"'.

These pouches or bags sometimes served as forels or covers for precious books some of which had embroidered covers. Jean, Duc de Berry, possessed a library of precious books, among which were bibles, psalters, breviaries and books of hours. Velvet in crimson and purple was a usual covering for such books. The duke possessed not only these but book covers in buff satin, blue silk and cloth of gold. Gold and silver thread were used to outline human figures and precious stones were set into the work. Borders were of leaves and of flowers and an old inventory states that 'Some were wrought with *fleurs de lys*, birds and images'.

A fine pouch at the cathedral treasury at Troyes may have served as a forel to a book with an embroidered cover; it dates from the first half of the thirteenth century and tradition holds that it was the property of Thibaut IV (known as the Singer), Count of Champagne. The direct influence of the East is apparent in the pictorial representation of a Saracen dressed in white, killing a lion reposing at the feet of Eleanor of Aquitaine. Coloured silks are used for the borders and scrolls but much of the work is in appliqué attached to a foundation of rich red velvet.

The main work in embroidery in France in the earlier Middle Ages was, as elsewhere in western Europe, devoted to the church. The designs were bold and spectacular as can be seen from the numerous garments which have been bequeathed from those days. It is probable that the designs were influenced strongly by the representations and colours shown on stained glass windows. There developed a tendency to group figures or motifs in quatrefoils which were later interlaced in patterns which in themselves contributed to the beauty of the whole.

Orphreys often bore the design of the Tree of Jesse whose figures and details appear to have been inspired by the earlier illuminated manuscripts. The stress on the sacred genealogy of Christ was acceptable to an age which emphasized family trees by representations on coats of arms. In the Tree of Jesse representations, an old and sleeping patriarch representing Abraham was often shown at the base of the trunk while David and Solomon were depicted on side branches. The figure of the Virgin Mary surmounted these and the topmost branch bore a crucifix. The technique approach to this design was to represent it in silk and satin, the latter proving particularly useful in the depicting of human flesh. Fine black silk was used for features, the thread being pulled to the back of the material in such a manner as to suggest that the features had been introduced with a fine paint brush. Backgrounds were beautiful in themselves, being worked in Hungarian stitch with gold thread.

Outstanding among church furnishings of the fourteenth century is an altar frontal kept at St Martin's Church in Liège. Dedicated to the Bishop of Tours, it shows scenes in the life of that saintly cleric and was probably designed by the more skilled of the contemporary artists of Tours. That period may be regarded as a golden age in that the

48

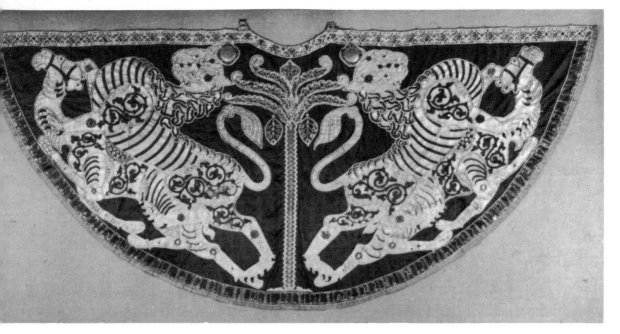

1 AUSTRIA Gold embroidered on pure silk, 12th century
Imperial Coronation robe
Kunsthistorisches Museum, Vienna. Heinz E. Kiewe Embroidery Collection, Oxford

2 ITALY Tree of Life, 12th century
Prototype design, probably Sicilian
Heinz E. Kiewe Embroidery Collection, Oxford

3 EGYPT Linen hanging, 4th–5th century
This hanging, embroidered with coloured wool is from the burying ground of Shuik Shata, Lower
Egypt. *Victoria and Albert Museum, London*

4 GREAT BRITAIN Panel, 13th century
The heraldic arms of Edward I and Queen Eleanor of Castile embroidered on shields; also the heraldic
bearings of Arundel, De Clare, De Vere and Hastings. Arcaded panels with powdering of crescent
moons and stars. *Metropolitan Museum of Art, New York. Gift of J. Pierpont Morgan, 1917*

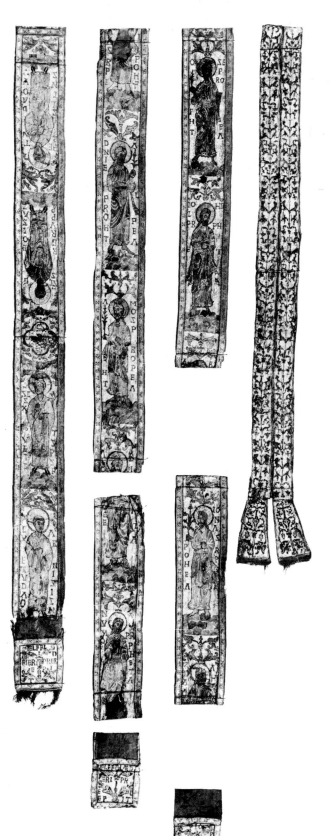

5 GREAT BRITAIN Stole of St Cuthbert, early 10th century
This stole is in several fragments *Durham Cathedral*

6 GREAT BRITAIN Band of cope, early 14th century
In an architectural framework are the figures of St James the Great and St John the Baptist. St James wears a long mantle of green and yellow. St John, by tradition wears a short mantle. Couching in gold, silver and coloured silks. *Brussels Museum*

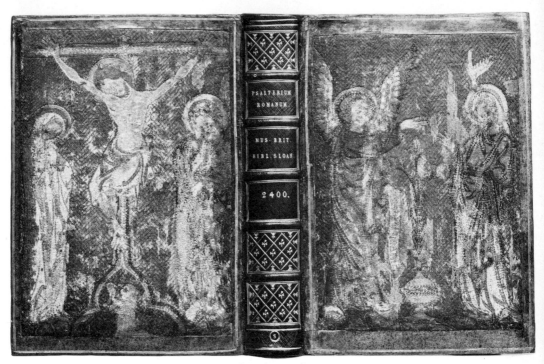

7 GREAT BRITAIN Cover of Felbrigge Psalter, late 13th century
Scenes show annunciation and crucifixion. Embroidery in gold and coloured silks on two-fold linen.
Background of surface-couched gold. *British Museum, London*

8 GREAT BRITAIN Panel; figure of St George on a horse (fragment), early 14th century
Original figure has been remounted on background of later date. Helmet of gold; armour black; red
crosses and dragons. Coloured silks and metallic threads. *Stonyhurst College, Lancashire*

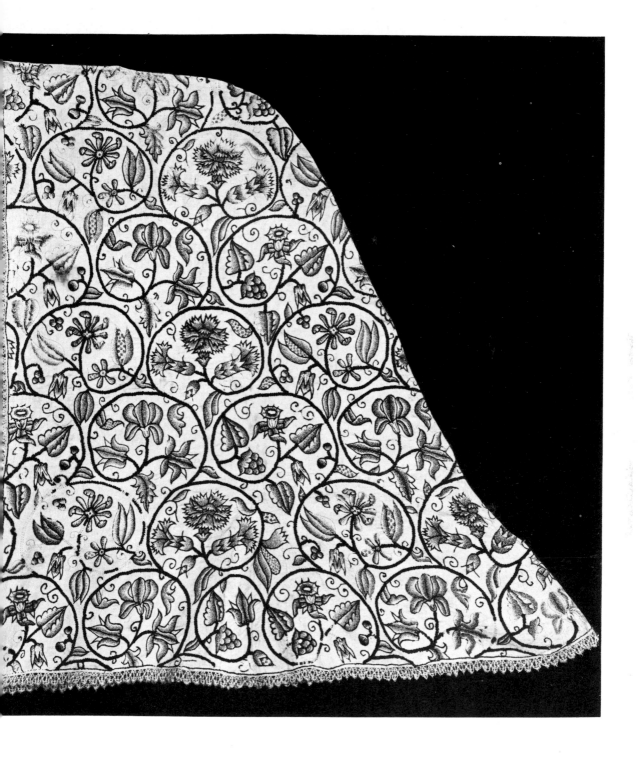

9   GREAT BRITAIN Lady's head-dress, 16th century
Embroidered in black silk and trimmed with bobbin lace
Victoria and Albert Museum, London

10 GREAT BRITAIN Book binding, 16th century
By tradition the handwork of Queen Elizabeth I. Ornamental filigree of gold and silver wire; groundwork of blue corded silk. Carries the initials K P (possibly Katherine Parr) in the centre of each cover.

Bodleian Museum, Oxford

11 GREAT BRITAIN Embroidered cushion, Elizabethan
Victoria and Albert Museum, London

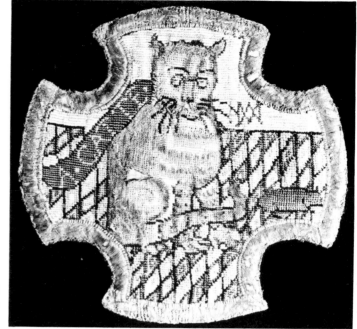

12 GREAT BRITAIN Panel (hanging fragment), 16th century
The Oxburgh Panel, attributed to Mary, Queen of Scots.

13 GREAT BRITAIN Picture, 16th century
Embroidery attributed to Mary, Queen of Scots; by tradition worked by the Queen when a prisoner in Bolton Castle.

Bolton Castle, Yorkshire

14 GREAT BRITAIN Tunic of The Black Prince
Replica of surcoat above his tomb (*c.* 1376) and made at the Royal School of Needlework, London in 1954.

Canterbury Cathedral

15 GREAT BRITAIN Embroidered box, 17th century   *Luton Museum*
Panels of embroidered work on wood base

16 NORWAY Silk skirt, mid 18th century   *Kunstindustrimuseet, Oslo*

17 GREAT BRITAIN Bodice (detail), 16th
century
Flower and fruit designs in black work
Embroiderers' Guild

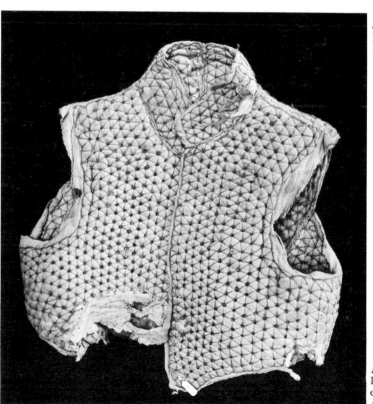

18 GREAT BRITAIN Jerkin, 16th century
Dagger proof; padded linen; quilt work and
embroidery.
Nottingham Museum, Middleton Collection

19 GREAT BRITAIN Casket, early
17th century
Stump work
Smithsonian Institution, Washington, DC

20 GREAT BRITAIN Jacket, 17th century
White linen, embroidered in silver thread
in chain stitch, with spangles.
Nottingham Museum, Middleton Collection

21 GREAT BRITAIN Portrait of Charles I,
c. 1660 (5 x 4⅛ in.)
Oval background of green satin. The king
wears a brown coat and a deep lace collar. The
whole surrounded by a silver rope.
Victoria and Albert Museum, London

22 GREAT BRITAIN Picture, 1610
Stump work
Frost and Reed, Bristol

23 GREAT BRITAIN Nightcaps, 17th century
Two nightcaps embroidered in black work. Characteristic scroll designs on linen.
Nottingham Museum, Middleton Collection

24 GREAT BRITAIN Pair of embroidered gloves, 17th century
Victoria and Albert Museum, London

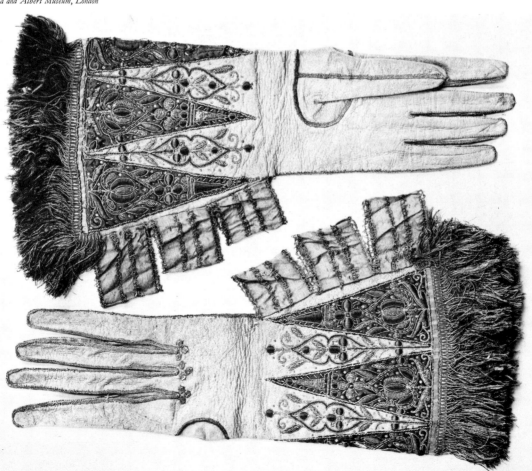

25   GREAT BRITAIN Dress, 17th century
Fabric of striped wool, embroidered with silver gilt threads.
Metropolitan Museum of Art, New York. Rogers Fund, 1933

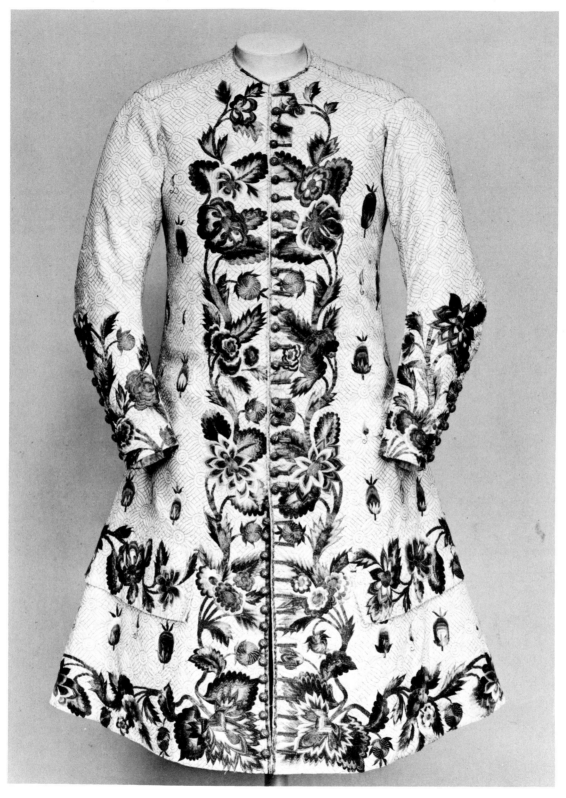

26 GREAT BRITAIN Jacket, early 18th century
Embroidered in pastel colours and silver gilt. Stitchery in pink, green, yellow and white on a linen foundation.

Metropolitan Museum of Art, New York. Rogers Fund, 1945

27 GREAT BRITAIN Stomacher, 17th century
Embroidered work on silk ground
City Art Gallery, Manchester

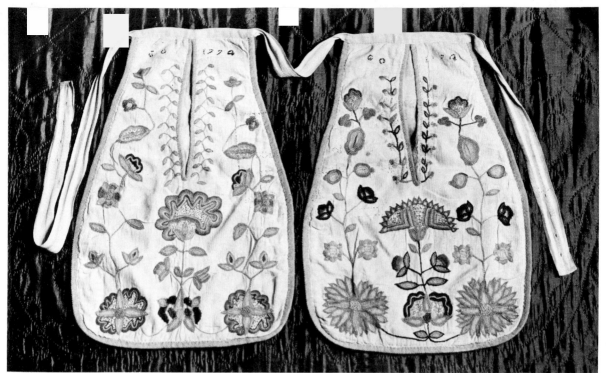

28 GREAT BRITAIN Pockets, 1774
Ribbed cotton, bound with woollen braid, embroidered in wool with chain stitch and satin stitch.
City Art Gallery, Manchester

29 GREAT BRITAIN Stomacher, early 18th century
Pink satin, embroidered in silk and metal thread, mainly in satin stitch and laid work.
City Art Gallery, Manchester

30 GREAT BRITAIN Georgian silk writing pad *c.* 1760
From the collection of writing pads belonging to the late Queen Mary.
Heinz E. Kiewe Embroidery Collection, Oxford

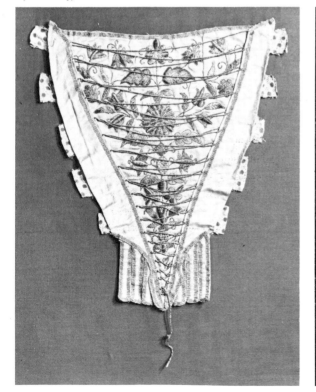

31 GREAT BRITAIN Armchair, *c.* 1750
Design shows a shepherd boy, a woman, a lion, dog and sheep. There are flowers and a scroll.

Lent by the Earl of Crawford and Balcarres. Heinz E. Kiewe Embroidry Collection, Oxford

32 GREAT BRITAIN Child's dress, 1860–70
White cotton with openwork embroidery (broderie anglaise)
City Art Gallery, Manchester

33 GREAT BRITAIN Needle etching on pure silk (style of T.G.Chalon R.A.) *c.* 1830
Pure silk thread and human hair give richness of texture. Approximately eight different strengths of thread have been used.
Heinz E. Kiewe Embroidery Collection, Oxford

34 GREAT BRITAIN
Dress, 1809
Muslin embroidered in metal
thread; chain stitch and
spangles.
City Art Gallery, Manchester

Below
35 GREAT BRITAIN
Boots, 1875–85
Embroidered with coloured
silks
City Art Gallery, Manchester

Opposite
36 GREAT BRITAIN
Smock (worn at Stewkley,
Buckinghamshire)   Linen;
opening in front and fastened
with brass buttons.
Right
Luton Museum

37 GREAT BRITAIN
Braces, early 19th century
Left braces worked in wool
on canvas lined with blue
silk; leather tabs (unworn).
Right braces embroidered in
tent stitch with floral design
in coloured silk on canvas;
elastic and kid straps. It was
the custom about 1800 for
young engaged women to
work such braces as gifts for
their friends.
Luton Museum

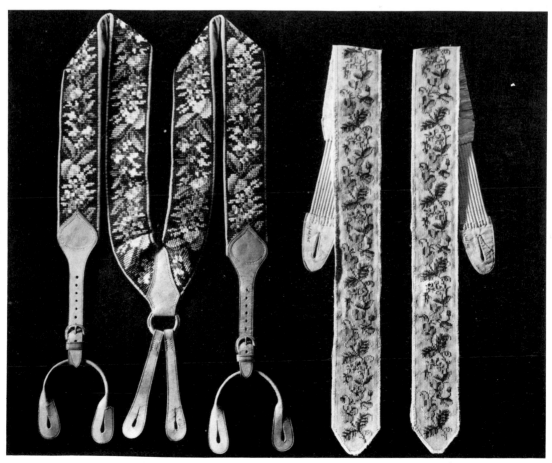

38 GREAT BRITAIN Chasuble, 1917
Worked by the Sisters of Bethany on cathedral damask.
Cirencester Cathedral

Below
39 GREAT BRITAIN Altar frontal, *c.* 1918
Designed by Sir Ninian Comper. Worked by the Sisters of Bethany as a war memorial.
Cirencester Cathedral (the Lady Chapel)

Opposite
40 GREAT BRITAIN Hand-embroidered picture against a silver metal background, by Pitt Henrich, 1968

41 GREAT BRITAIN Toy Embroidered felt
National Federation of Women's Institutes

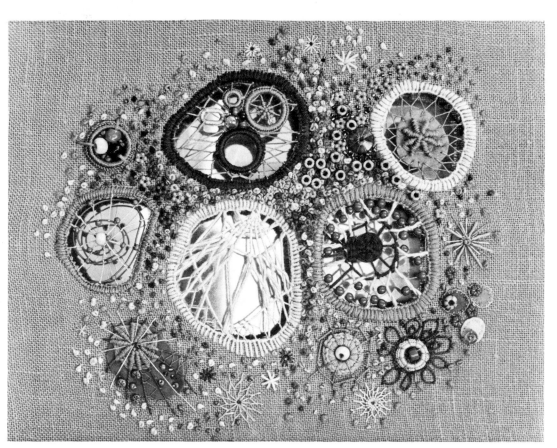

42 FRANCE Panel, late 18th century
For the back of a chair
Victoria and Albert Museum, London

43 FRANCE Train of a robe, 1855
Gazelin, Paris. White twilled silk embossed in gold thread.
Victoria and Albert Museum, London

44 FRANCE Apparel for a dalmatic, 16th century
Satin applied to velvet

Victoria and Albert Museum, London

45 FRANCE Bag, early 20th century
Modern work incorporating appliqué

Glasgow College of Art

46   GERMANY Orphrey from the back
of a chasuble (Westphalia), 15th century
Embroidered linen
Victoria and Albert Museum, London

47 GERMANY Embroidered cover on silk ground, 1620
Design shows Renaissance influence
Victoria and Albert Museum, London

48 GERMANY Embroidered muslin (Saxony), 18th century
Victoria and Albert Museum, London

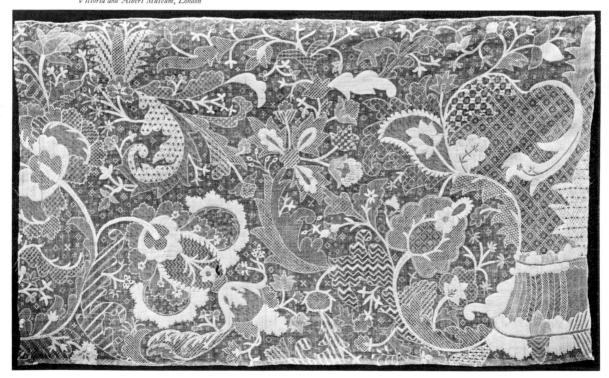

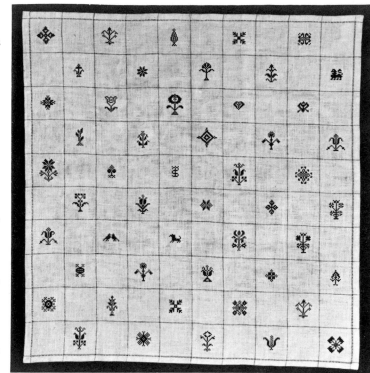

49 SWITZERLAND Floral motifs in cross stitch on fine linen. Modern.
Glasgow College of Art

50 FINLAND Runner in fine lawn, early 20th century
Victoria and Albert Museum, London

51 NORWAY Tea cloth, early 20th century
Drawn thread work on fine cloth.
Victoria and Albert Museum, London

52 DENMARK Tea cosy and tray cloth, early 20th century
Glasgow College of Art

50   51   52

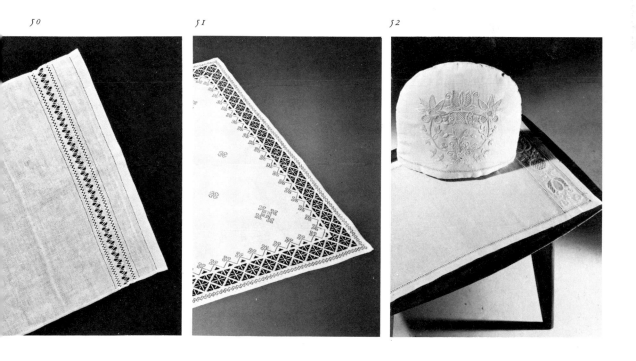

53 ITALY Cope (detail), late 13th century
The Coronation of the Virgin. In the detail Christ and the Virgin are seated facing each other; Christ's hand is raised, in blessing. Saint Peter, on the right, holds two large keys, one silver and one gold.
Vatican Museum, Rome

54 ITALY Panel of embroidered coverlet (Florence), 15th century
Victoria and Albert Museum, London

55 ITALY Panels of embroidered work (Florence), 15th century
Victoria and Albert Museum, London

56 ITALY Embroidered panel, early 20th century
Glasgow College of Art

57 SPAIN Panel, 16th century
In cross stitch
Victoria and Albert Museum, London

58 SPAIN Panel, 16th century
In red and black. Bird motifs; embroidered in
Mexico.
Glasgow College of Art

59 AUSTRIA Viennese petit point, *c.* 1816

Heinz E. Kiewe Embroidery Collection, Oxford

Worked in pure silk

60 SPAIN Altar frontal (Spanish work), 17th century
Six scenes are from the life of St Theresa. Flower and fruit motifs.

Salisbury Cathedral

61 PORTUGAL Embroidered panel, 1725
Victoria and Albert Museum, London

62 PORTUGAL Apron, 1896
Embroidered work on plain and gathered
grounds
Glasgow College of Art

63 FLANDERS Hood of a cope, late 15th century
Victoria and Albert Museum, London

64 FLANDERS
Orphrey, early 16th century
From the back of a chasuble. Silk stitching on linen.

Victoria and Albert Museum, London

65 AUSTRIA Panel, *c.* 1825
Showing leaf and fruit design worked in long and short stitch
Glasgow College of Art

66 POLAND Cushion cover, *c.* 1870
Showing cross stitch
Victoria and Albert Museum, London

67 YUGOSLAVIA Tunic, late 19th century
With front panels and borders embroidered in coloured silks
Glasgow College of Art

68 HUNGARY Embroidered blouse, late 19th century
Showing panels in drawn thread work, silk embroidery and lace trimmings

Glasgow College of Art

69 CZECHOSLOVAKIA Child's dress, mid 19th century
Front, sleeves and cuffs show coloured embroidery on white ground

Glasgow College of Art

70 GREAT BRITAIN Embroidered apron, 1730–1750
City Art Gallery, Manchester

71   GREAT BRITAIN The travellers; the children from
Chaucer's Tales, 1966
Crewel embroidery on linen twill designed and em-
broidered by Joyce Knowles
Heinz E. Kiewe Embroidery Collection, Oxford

72   USA Costumes 19th and 20th centuries
Two dresses. Simple dress for woman and child. Empire
period wedding dress.
Smithsonian Institution, Washington, DC

73 DENMARK White embroidery on a
ground of fine texture, *c.* 1890
Glasgow College of Art

74 NORWAY Bag, 1887
Wool embroidery
Glasgow College of Art

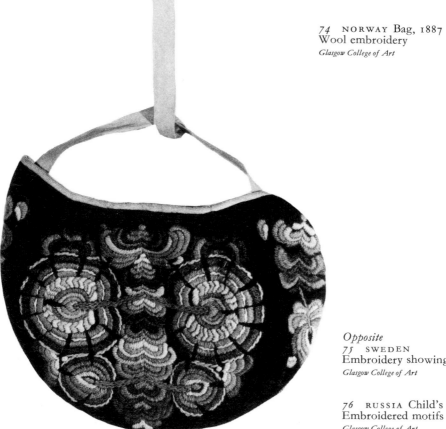

Opposite
75 SWEDEN
Embroidery showing floral design
Glasgow College of Art

76 RUSSIA Child's silk skirt, 1877
Embroidered motifs
Glasgow College of Art

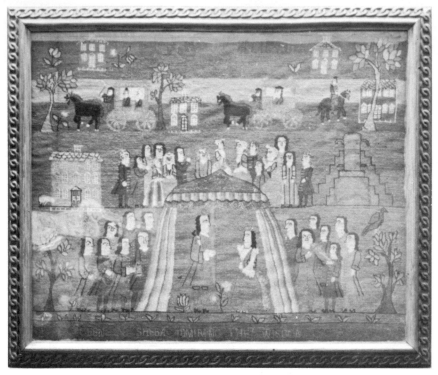

77 USA Petit point needlework 'The Queen of Sheba and Solomon', 1744, Massachusetts
Smithsonian Institution, Washington, DC

78 USA Crewel work and needle point, examples of various articles enriched with embroidery, 18th century
Top row, from left to right:
Crewel embroidered bed valance, *c.* 1750
Crewel work pocket cover, 1736
Fragment of crewel work (in a frame). Late 17th century, or early 18th century
Lady's pocketbook. Crewel work on wool. Mid 18th century.
Bottom row, left to right:
Crewel embroidered curtain fragments
Man's flame stitch needlework pocketbook
Pellise crewel, embroidered at border, 1797
Smithsonian Institute, Washington, DC

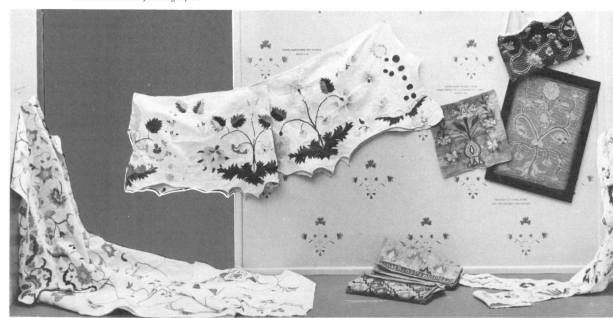

80 USA Bill book, 18th century

79 USA Bill book, late 18th century
Made at Bethel, Maine. Materials locally raised and woven.

81 USA Embroidered fragment of
pocketbook, 18th century

82 USA Silk burse by
Mrs Bucky King
Only metal threads used
Embroideries Unlimited, Pittsburgh

83 USA Silk chalice veil
by Mrs Bucky King
Appliqué and metal
thread work
Embroideries Unlimited, Pittsburgh

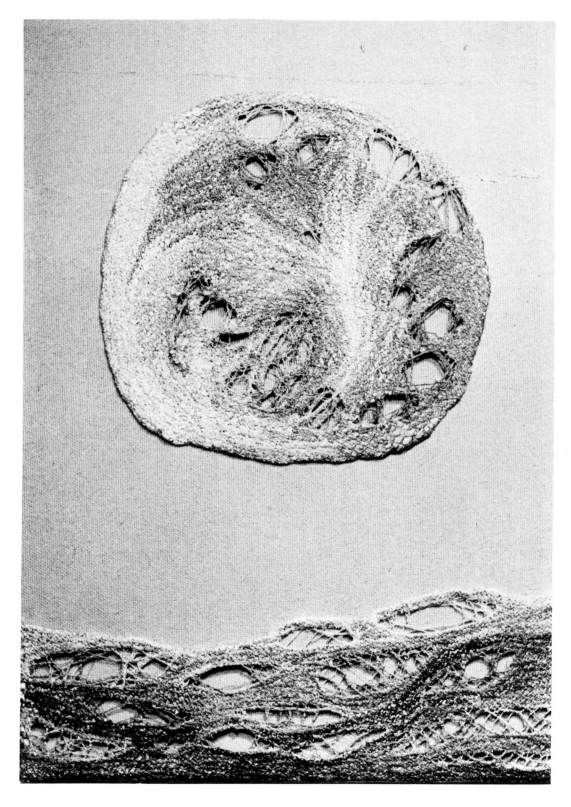

84 USA 'Earth' by Everett K. Sturgeon, Oakdale
Free machine embroidery
Embroideries Unlimited, Pittsburgh

85 GREAT BRITAIN Collage by Alison Taylor
Hand embroidery with appliqué plus surface stitches

designer, equally at home in the arts of embroidery, illuminating and painting, had practical and sure knowledge of his media, their possibilities and their limitations.

Ecclesiastical accessories received careful attention in France. Some beautiful mitres have been bequeathed from the Middle Ages. Caen, noted for its embroidered pouches, was commissioned in 1481 by Charles of Neufchatel to embroider a mitre which he presented to the cathedral of Besançon. The work was undertaken and the design created in coloured silks, gold thread and precious stones.

At the museum at Cluny there are several beautiful mitres of this period. One of the finest is at the church of St Gildas de Ruys in the Mohriban district. It dates from the fifteenth century and most of the work is in appliqué on a silk ground. The figures represented are those of two abbots who are probably patrons of the priory. In this case, the lappets of the mitre are also embroidered for on one side is depicted a martyr who has been beheaded and he is shown as having been burnt at the stake. The other lappet bears the figure of St Sebastian and he is shown dying, pierced with an arrow.

A survey of the mitres shows that they too were subject to changes in fashion. At first they were small and low but in the fifteenth century they grew to sizes which were almost monstrous. At that period they became curved and the sharp angles, which had characterized earlier mitres, fell into disuse.

Ecclesiastical gloves were adorned with some of the finest of the embroiderers' work. Designs were delicate and stitchery exquisite and there was a predilection for arabesques and interlacing scrolls. Mittens appear to have formed part of ecclesiastical costume and an inventory of Bayeux Cathedral refers to 'two woollen mittaynes with embroidery on the hands with two figures of St Veronica surrounded by pearls'.

Of the main garments of ecclesiastical wear, France produced some of the finest in western Europe, particularly in the fourteenth and fifteenth centuries. What was known as 'the Great Embroidery' belonged to the cathedral at Angers. It was the gift in 1462 of René d'Anjou, King of Sicily, and represented the work of a famous embroiderer from Avignon, Pierre du Vaillant, a man already famous as a painter. The set of embroideries comprised a tunic, a chasuble, a dalmatic and a cope and also an altar hanging. The latter was in velvet and bore the coat of arms of René d'Anjou and his wife Isabella and on panels of gold were designs showing angels, symbols of the mediaeval church and crowns. The ecclesiastical garments carried designs representing scenes in the life of St Maurice, the patron of the cathedral, while powderings of flowers adorned the groundwork of the garments.

Another chasuble of late fifteenth century date belongs to Naintré, near Chatellerault, in the department of Vienne. The design on the orphrey shows St Thomas and other saints symbolized according to mediaeval iconography.

The princes and nobles prided themselves on their patronage of the arts and where the royal court travelled, skilled embroiderers gathered. The names of some of these workers have reached us across the centuries, among them being those of Colin Jolye and Simonne de Gaules, embroiderers at Brouges when Charles VII was resident there.

Louis XI, when he established his court at Tours, encouraged the development of the textile industry and patronized the art of embroidery, giving personal commission to Jehan de Moucy. The kingly interest extended as far as the cultivation of mulberry trees and the importation in 1470 of Italian craftsmen including 'a silk trimmer, a dyer, a thread spinner and a gold thread drawer'.

Avignon became a centre of culture under Gregory X and textiles benefited from the close proximity to Italy. Embroiderers in particular flourished in Avignon and it was in the workshops of this city that 'the Great Embroidery' associated with Angers Cathedral was made.

There was a further influx of Italian workers in and around 1494 when Charles VIII returned from a victorious campaign in Sicily and Naples. Philip de Commines refers to 'the many workmen excelling in divers crafts... whom the king brought back from Italy'. These immigrations are noteworthy and in them may be found the foundations of the blending of French and Italian tastes which characterized so trenchantly the embroidery work of the sixteenth century. The influence of Italy was then strengthened during the time of the Medicis under whose rule France progressed into the richness of the Renaissance period.

Embroidery tended to supersede fur in secular costume as the mediaeval period advanced. Pearls were used lavishly to adorn clothing. Quicherat in his *Histoire du Costume* relates how in 1414 Charles of Orleans ordered a greatcoat adorned with nine hundred and sixty pearls. On the sleeves were embroidered the verses of a folk song *Madame, I am joyous*, together with the notes of music. The staves were represented in gold thread and each note was marked with four pearls. Notes were shown in square shape at the time.

Spangles were also used freely with embroidery to adorn costume. An account book of 1389 carries an entry relating to 'iij marcs xvijs esterlins of fine gold at xxij carats, delivered at Estienne d'Epernon, gold beater, to be flattened and shaped into broom blossoms for stitching on to two embroidered doublets of the King.'

Scrolls of gold and tiny rings of gold and silver were used to the number of thousands on the garments of the nobility. Such was the extravagance of secular costume that Philippe le Bel issued in 1294 a sumptuary law limiting the wearing of embroidered garments to royal princes. It was almost traditional, however, to ignore such laws.

Accessories of dress and also shoes, gloves and head-dresses were embroidered too and articles of furniture were enhanced with embroidered textiles. The furnishings of a mediaeval castle included numerous wall hangings and curtains which served to partition off the larger rooms. Beds, for instance, required curtains to shield their occupants from severe draughts and canopies were called into use at social functions. Labarthe quotes an inventory of the reign of Charles V wherein are described details of such furnishings.

ITEM   A tent of French embroidery in which are depicted the four evangelists in a framework of architectural shapes with curtains striped in green and purple and rayed with gold.

ITEM   A chamber hung with cloth of gold on which is a bright red velvet cross embroidered with coats of arms.

ITEM   A chamber hung with cloth of silver ornamented with five compass devices embroidered with the arms of France, the Dauphin; also a canopy or tester, hanging draperies for head board and counterpane or coverlet and three curtains of Indian cendel.

Such furnishings were carried from castle to castle and special carved coffers or chests were made for this purpose. A king travelling from one town to another often took several of these coffers with him. Several must have been used for Queen Joan of Burgundy when she travelled to Rheims for the coronation celebrations, for her room at the palace had sumptuous furnishings.

The mediaeval embroideries of France have much of the sweetness and grace which one almost expects of the country. This was evident in secular as well as ecclesiastical work and these qualities were to develop to the full in the Renaissance period.

The Renaissance period of French embroidery

A distinct advance in the technique of embroidery was evident early in the Renaissance years. France benefited from the direct tuition of Italian embroiderers. Fortunately she preserved her own individuality and expressed this in her textiles (plate 44).

There was a general raising of standards of life with the coming of the Renaissance and embroiderers found that their work was open to criticism from a discriminating laity. The bold effects of the Middle Ages were discarded in favour of more subtle work revealing fineness of execution and subtle gradations of colours which were blended happily. In efforts to portray human flesh, embroiderers at times abandoned the needle for the paint brush; others, with more harmonious results, achieved their effects with delicate silks and split stitches. The vigilance of the Corporation of Embroiderers of Paris and the importance laid on the representing of flesh realistically is apparent in a promulgation issued in 1551 which ordained that 'the colouring in representation of nude figures and faces should be done in three or four gradations of carnation dyed silk and not as formerly in white silks'.

Growing interest in the creation of lace did not diminish interest in the craft of embroidery. The status of embroidery work may be inferred from the fact that the chief artists of the time created designs to be worked in silks and kindred threads. Raphael (1483–1520) was commissioned by Francis I to prepare a pattern for embroidery and this may still be seen in the Cluny Museum. The oval medallion is part of a set of furnishings for the coronation chamber of the king. The set included a table cover, a fire screen, covers for four armchairs, eighteen folding stools and also bed curtains. It is known that the room was also decorated with scenes from the history of the Jews and the textile furnishings were preserved in the Abbey of St Denis until the French Revolution, but the medallion at Cluny is the sole fragment which survived a holocaust of the embroideries. It shows a scene representing the Israelites worshipping the golden calf, the whole being worked on a gold ground.

Much of the work of the early period of the Renaissance was done on canvas for linen was rare and expensive. Applied canvas work and tent stitch were usual. As the sixteenth century advanced, linen came into more general use not only for personal attire but for household purposes. Table covers, towels and table napkins were now embroidered and pleasing effects were produced with borders of red silk.

The introduction of white linen led to the development of cut work or *point coupé* which in turn orientated towards needlepoint lace. Drawn work (*à fils tirés*) was another expression of the prevailing taste for delicate fabric.

The new modes demanded new designs, the embroiderers could no longer turn to old specimens nor to those motifs recorded on samplers and had, at first, to resort to ingenuity. Then they passed on and developed the patterns they had created. Later the printing press came to their help. In addition, embroidery patterns which owed much to the early wood engravings were circulated and designs now took on an international aspect.

European embroidery had designs which were universal.

Pattern makers were many and included Pelegrin, Vosterman, Tagliente, Lepince, Aristotile, Guadignino and others scattered throughout France. Some of the designs could be used for needle point lace but some of the pattern makers restricted themselves expressly to embroidery. Pierre Quinty whose pattern book appeared in 1527 appears to have eschewed the art of lace-making, for the title of his book proclaims it to be *A New and Subtle Book, sponsoring the Art and Science of making Embroidery, Fringes, Tapestries.*

The craft of embroidery was held in high esteem and received the direct patronage of the royal court. Catherine de' Medici was skilled with her needle and taught the princesses of the court, including Mary, Queen of Scots, the intricacies of the craft.

Patrons of embroidery commissioned needleworkers to make embroideries which were not only ambitious but often ludicrous. The embroiderers accepted the challenge and thus as the seventeenth century evolved an unhealthy style developed. Nevertheless the work was done with such excellence that the depravity of taste and the mixing of media are sometimes glossed over by the high standard of execution.

Quicherat in his *Histoire du Costume* testifies to the important part played by embroidery in the ornamentings of costume. Garments were of velvet. Borders, insertions and panels were of embroidery showing scrolls, arabesques, fruits, dolphins and interlaced cyphers. Shirts of Holland or linen were much valued. These received their share of embroidery as did also stockings of wool.

Internecine religious strife in the reign of Charles IX did not cancel out the extravagances of the royal court. A petition presented to Catherine de' Medici from a gentleman of Bordeaux complains of the nobility and states that 'their lands, their pastures, their woods and all their revenues are wasted upon embroideries, insertions, trimmings, tassels, fringes, needleworks... new diversities of which are invented from day to day'.

The extravagances of the court were intensified yet further in the reign of Henry III. A young 'blood' prided himself on his elegant costume adorned with embroideries, the designs of which were reproduced in the metal work of his sword, dagger and scabbard.

Reminiscent of the Flemish Order of the Golden Fleece was the Order of the Saint Esprit founded by Henry III on 31 December 1578. The knights were dressed in red velvet embroidered with gold thread and the crests of the order were worked in gold on the garments. Priests were appointed to minister to the Order and the ecclesiastical garments worn were also richly embroidered.

The seventeenth century witnessed a vogue for brocades and kindred ornate materials and the fashion for velvet passed. The new materials were ornate in themselves but they were embroidered with exotic designs of plants and fruits. Jean Robin, a horticulturist, was also an opportunist and his Jardin des Plantes provided unusual specimens which embroiderers could copy. The garden later became crown property under Henry IV, and a centre for students studying medicine, and embroidery became subservient to science.

The simplicity-loving Henry IV issued edicts against the wearing of extravagant costume. These appear to have had but little effect for Louis XIII was obliged to issue in 1629 an edict on 'Superfluity in Clothes'. Sections of this law referred to embroidery.

'We forbid men and women to wear in any way whatsoever embroidery on cloth or flax, imitations of embroidery, of bordering made up with cloth and thread and of cutwork for capes, sleeves... and other linens.'

An effort was made to foster home industries by the enactment.

'And we forbid the use of all other ornaments upon capes, sleeves and other linen garments, save trimmings, cutwork and laces manufactured in this country who do not exceed at most the price of three pounds the ell, that is for the band and its trimmings together without evasion.'

The engravings of Abraham Bosse show the men and women of fashion of the time bedizened with all manner of extravagant ornamentations and these illustrations are evidence that Louis' edict was ignored.

The reign of Louis XIV marks an epoch in the history of France. During that long period, the royal court at Versailles became the centre of luxury in Europe.

The king was an ardent patron of embroidery. His taste is questioned today when it is recalled that in his palace he had caryatid figures in gold embroidery accentuated in relief. The medium, according to present day verdict, was unsuitable but the figures, measuring fifteen feet high, were acclaimed at the time, St Aubin declaring them to be 'specimens of masterwork beyond eulogy'.

Louis had a band of personal embroiderers in his household and eminent among them were Rémy, Jean Henry and Etienne Henry and also Jean le Bayteau. There were craftsmen also at the Gobelins factory where royal tapestries were made. Among the embroiderers engaged there were Balland and Simon Fayette who worked harmoniously in the embroidering of furnishing materials. Fayette's pictorial scenes and figures were placed in Balland's landscape settings. The Gobelins factory could command the help of the first-class artists of the time and their names appear frequently in the account books relating to commissioned work.

> To Boulogne, for drawings of birds and flowers 72 livres [about £3]
> To Balland, for embroideries representing the capturing of birds in flight, 200 livres
> To Balland for embroidered landscapes 2855 livres
> To Fayette for figures embroidered 2345 livres
> To Bonneur painter for six paintings upon vellum to be used as patterns for embroideries on furniture in the gallery at Versailles 300 livres
> To Tastelin for a painting of Jupiter on his eagle for use as a pattern for embroidery 300 livres.

The Grand Monarch can be expected to have inspired a grand style. The more graceful forms of the previous reigns were abandoned for grandiose emblems showing royal suns, diadems, pennons.

Portraits painted in this reign including those by Rigaud and engravings by Gautier, Simon and others show with remarkable detail the use of embroidery on contemporary costume. Judging from such evidence and from literary accounts, it becomes clear that women showed a more refined taste than men for they favoured the use of the more delicate and restrained linens and lawns which were gaining popularity. If Madame de Sévigné's fluent jocularity is representative of the women of her time, the ladies found the costumes of the men fecund objects of fun.

'M. de Langlée has given M. de Montespan a costume of gold upon gold, wrought over with gold with hems of gold. Then over it is a curling additional embroidery of one gold mixed with another certain gold, making altogether the most divine fabric that I could possibly have imagined!! Fairies certainly made all this in secret.'

The royal court continued to patronize the craft of embroidery. Mme de Maintenon taught the art at the college which she established at St Cyr. Here, during an apprenticeship lasting three years, girls of noble blood were engaged in embroidering hangings for Fontainebleau and other royal palaces. Oriental motifs were influencing designs and trade with the East was intensified under Colbert. The practice of sending materials to China to to be embroidered spread through the country but the craft of embroidery did not lapse at home.

The interest of the royal mistress in embroidered furnishings for the royal palaces was in the tradition set by earlier queens. Bonnaffé in his researches on Catherine de' Medici discovered details concerning the mourning bed acquired by the queen on the death of her husband in 1559. This bed was placed in the queen's bedroom which had a border of cloth of silver ornamented with emblems in black appliqué. An adjoining dressing-room had hangings of black satin embroidered in white. The bed itself was of 'black velvet, embroidered with pearls, powdered with crescents and suns, a footboard, headboard and nine valances and coverlet of state, similarly bedecked with crescents and suns, three damask curtains with leafy wreaths and garlands figured upon a gold and silver ground and fringed along the edges with broderies of pearls'.

Renaissance interest was centred in embroidery pictures and these figure prominently in French inventories. The close analogy between embroidery and painting was apparent to Laborde when he wrote in *La Renaissance des Arts à la Tour de France*. 'The art of embroidery became a serious and esteemed sister of painting, for the needle, in truth a painter's brush, traversed its canvas, leaving behind it a dyed thread as a colour, producing a painting soft in tone, ingenious in touch – a picture without glistening surface, brilliant without harshness.'

Many of these pictures, judging from the descriptions contained in inventories, were portraits of royal and noble personages. Other showed scriptural scenes. A few that have survived are of especial interest as they are contemporary records of dress and amusements; one such picture shows a scene at the royal court and is a representation of a bear fight attended by Henry II and Diane de Poitiers. Figures and perspective are true and life-like effects are achieved by fine stitchery in silk.

It is highly probable that the foremost artists of the time prepared either directly or indirectly the designs for the embroidered pictures. A needlework picture representing Christ, at Lyons Museum, is reminiscent of the work of Rembrandt.

The Victoria and Albert Museum is fortunate in the possession of a small embroidered picture inspired by a design created by the Florentine painter, del Garbo. It depicts a saint reading the gospels. He is seated in an alcove and holds a cross in his hand.

A small casket in the same museum is also of French work. The design resembles those used for embroidered pictures. Twelve panels are arranged on the casket which is fourteen and three quarter inches long and the emblems on these refer to the twelve months of the year. The signs of the zodiac are introduced and inscriptions are added in French. Relief is introduced by means of padding and details of architecture are emphasized with metallic thread. Faces and certain details are made with long and short stitches and gold cord is used for outlines.

The needlework pictures of the Renaissance period have undoubted charm and individuality. The needleworker was not limited so strictly as the tapestry weaver for the textures of the materials to hand had intrinsic qualities contributing to light and shade effects. When allied to a design of good taste, the needle paintings of France were objects of artistic worth and real charm.

From the eighteenth century to the present day

The brilliant period of the Renaissance had flourished in the Age of the Enlightened Despot. With the passing of Louis XIV a period of decadence set in, in all forms of French expression. The grandiose style, so characteristic of the Sun King, was eclipsed in the reign of Louis XV and descended to frippery. Oriental trends continued and were apparent in furnishing and costumes. So eager were many of the aristocrats that their clothing should be embroidered in the best Indian and Chinese taste that, according to St Aubin, many sent their garments to the East to be embroidered. Coats and waistcoats of the reigns of Louis XV and Louis XVI were ornamented in this manner.

Keen competition arose between men in sartorial affairs. Clothing was embroidered lavishly with sprays of flowers and similar designs. Meticulous attention was given to the decorating of cuffs, buttonholes and similar accessories, many of which are regarded today as being essentially feminine. Embroidery stitches were used in all varieties and textures; floss and spun silks were used for the purpose and the designs were accentuated with beads, spangles and silk threads manufactured into gimps, ribbons and chenille. Fantastic as were many of the masculine costumes, those of the women were more so. Quicherat relates the development of women's dress and the absurd proportions introduced into skirts and petticoats which were supported with hoops. Paris was now the recognized centre of fashion and what the women of that city wore was copied assiduously in many European countries and in America. Cambrics and muslin were favoured and all women's garments were embroidered. Petticoats, capes, pelerines, collars, gloves, hats and veils were ornamented with silks. Lace too was an essential trimming, its popularity growing greater as the eighteenth century advanced.

The authors of *Needlework through the Ages* quote a description written by Nollekens, the English sculptor, in which he gives an account of the wedding dress of his bride. For the wedding 'she wore a sacque petticoat of most expensive brocade in white silk resembling net-work, enriched with small flowers which displayed in variations of the folds a most delicate shade of pink, the uncommon beauty of which was greatly admired. The deep and pointed stomacher was exquisitely gimped and pinked; and at a lower part was a large pin, consisting of several diamonds, confining an elegant lace point apron'.

The same authors quote a description of a design on a black velvet petticoat worn at the wedding of the daughter of George II to the Prince of Orange. The petticoat was 'embroidered with chenille, the pattern a large stone vase filled with ramping flowers, that spread almost over a breadth of the petticoat from the bottom to the top; between each vase was a pattern of gold shells and foliage, embossed, and most heavily rich; the gown was white satin, embroidered also with chenille mixed with gold ornaments, no vases on the sleeve but two or three upon the tail'.

From the pen of a French writer in *Souvenirs de la Marquise de Créguy* comes an account of the costume worn by the Duchess de la Ferté. The dress was of rich red velvet. The folds of the ample skirt were held in position by brooches of Dresden china made in the semblance of butterflies. On a front panel of the dress was embroidered a design showing an orchestra complete with musical instruments. The latter were worked in relief and the musicians embroidered on cloth of silver were arranged in six rows. Within the skirt was a hoop of nearly six yards in circumference.

Royal and noble patronage was bestowed directly on embroiderers. Royal weddings were occasions for the lavish display of rich clothing. Leading artists such as Perreux, La Fage and Trumeau were engaged to design embroideries on the costumes worn at the wedding of the Grand Dauphin. Louis XV's revival of the Order of the Grand Esprit was also characterized by a splendid display of embroideries and it is recorded that a skilled embroiderer named Rocher was called upon to embroider the throne of the king. He in turn commissioned three hundred workmen to embroider the seat of honour and its accompanying hangings. Much of the work was done in gold thread and the ground-work of rich silk was powdered with *fleurs-de-lys*. Workmen also embroidered the uni-forms of the members of the Order and the vestments of the officiating clergy.

The rococo style displayed in embroideries on costumes found expression also in the furnishings of the period of Louis XV. France was the chief country in Europe in the manufacture of furnishings (plate 42) for she had direct access to rich textiles, tapestries, silks and lace. She had suffered a severe loss in the emigration of silk throwers and weavers to neighbouring countries following on the Revocation of the Edict of Nantes in 1685 but she retained powerful resources. Bezon in his *Dictionnaire des Tissus* has given an authoritative account of these and has described the prosperity of the silk industry at Lyons where designers and embroiderers also foregathered. Linen manufacture was fostered also at Cambrai, Valenciennes, Lille and St Quentin and the embroidering of muslin and cambrics led to an orientation away from embroideries in floss and twisted silks. The white embroideries of Saxony enjoyed a great, if passing, vogue.

The reign of Louis XIV (1638–1715) had witnessed an advance towards more luxurious furniture. This continued in the reign of Louis XV and his comfort-loving subjects re-joiced in chairs with stuffed and padded seats, sofas, causeries and day beds. Coverings were often of canvas adorned with cross and tent stitches which were easy to work but although the results of this technique were attractive, they cannot be classed as artistic. Under Louis XIV especially, designs were free and bold consisting mainly of flower mo-tifs. These were also used in the reign of Louis XV but the designs degenerated and incorporated innovations such as the figures of clowns and courtiers, shepherds and shepherdesses surrounded by exotic birds, ferocious dragons and mischievous monkeys.

Bed furnishings were excellent vehicles for the display of embroideries in an age when the *levée* was an occasion for a social gathering. The bed of Queen Marie Leczinska was embroidered with figures from classical history. Appliqué work was used extensively on bed coverings. Louis XV himself could claim skill of a high standard as an embroiderer and declared that none of his subjects could surpass him in the craft.

Royal patronage continued under Louis XVI and designers such as Salembier created floral designs of a more worthy nature than those made in the previous reign. There was a pleasing union of Renaissance motifs and classical figures, all worked on rich satins and silks. Interest in canvas work continued and was a fashionable occupation among aristocratic ladies. Queen Marie Antoinette was engaged in creating hangings in this medium for the Louvre. The reign indicated a return to a purer style but progress was cut short by the Revolution. Specimens of work that have survived show a fine and exacting taste. The work of G. Jacob, an *ébé-niste* or cabinet maker employed by the unfortunate Louis XVI, is now at Windsor Castle complete with its furnishings and coverings in satin embroidered with multi-coloured silks.

The destruction of the Revolution was wanton. It extended to degrees hard to credit. Old embroideries were unpicked by workwomen employed for the purpose. No trace of designs created under the old régime was to survive. There also arose the practice of 'parfilage' a custom known to other European countries also and referred to in England as 'drizzling'. Gold and other metallic threads were unravelled from old embroideries and placed in smelting pots for the good of impoverished nations. 'Parfilage' or 'drizzling' also assumed the form of a patriotic occupation among the ruling classes. At a fashionable gathering ladies assembled with their old specimens of embroidery and drizzling tools carried in special boxes and bags made for the purpose.

Napoleon patronized the industries of France and gave direct support to the crafts of lace and embroideries but the wars of the Empire cut short any ambitions he may have entertained in this sphere.

The more democratic trends of nineteenth century France resulted in the use of embroidered garments by all classes of society. The influence of the East was direct and France imported most beautiful exquisitely embroidered textiles. The French people in particular were attracted by the richness of the oriental crafts. Didron in his *Report on the Decorative Arts*, 1878, quotes Théophile Gautier's account in *L'Orient à l'Exposition* of an Indian embroidery.

> It might almost be said that Indian embroidery seeks to engage in a contest with the sun, to have a duel to the death with the blinding light and glowing sky; it attempts to shine brilliantly beneath his fiery deluge; it realizes the wonders of the fairy balls; it produces dresses in colours of the weather, of the sun, of the moon, metals, flowers, precious stones, lustres, beams of light and flashes are mixed upon its incandescent palette. Over a silvery net it makes wings of beetles to vibrate like fluttering golden emerald. With the scales of beetles' bodies, it gives birth to impossible foliage mixed with flowers of diamonds. It avails itself of the shimmer of tawny silk, of the opalescent hues of mother of pearl, of the splendid gold blue blendings of the peacock's plumage. It disdains nothing, not even tinsel, provided it flashes brightly, not even crystal as long as it radiates light. At all costs its duty is to shine and glitter and to send forth the prismatic rays; it must be blazing, blinding and phosphorescent – and so the sun acknowledges its defeat.

In the face of the importation of rich oriental embroideries, much of what was best in French textile crafts was neglected. As in England, much embroidery work was done but it was not in the best of taste and one of its most essential features was the necessity that it could be accomplished quickly. Furthermore, there was a deterioration in that embroidery work was now the result of cheap labour and embroideries were created with little regard to their ultimate use. The coming of the machine age was a further blow to artistic handicrafts.

Once the creation of machine-made goods was established, a reaction arose among the discriminating in favour of hand-made embroideries (plate 43). This resulted at first in copyings of earlier specimens. Although this imitation of age-old specimens was not altogether satisfactory, it possessed inherent virtues in that it made the artistically conscious aware of the possibilities of their craft. Thanks to skilful guidance, later French embroiderers advanced, as in other European countries, from the stage of reproduction to new and more individual work. In the technical exactitude of such work and the intense interest in design lie portents for a happy future in the world of embroidery.

6 Germany

Opus Teutonicum

The embroidery of Germany shows the existence of two distinct movements. One was the expression of the nobility and burghers together with the town guilds and has much in common with work produced by similar communities elsewhere in Europe. The other was an expression of peasant achievement. The latter was not, in its final evaluation, subsidiary to the former. Its virility is evident to this day. The Austrian Professor Haberlandt has written trenchantly in its defence. 'Rural art,' he says, 'is by no means an undeveloped branch of art in general. Ancient traditions and even what may be termed prehistoric influences, can be traced into it; not to a superior civilization does it owe its form or technique; far oftener than these, to an ancient heritage faithfully preserved.'

The embroideries of the German-speaking countries of the Middle Ages have, fortunately, been catalogued precisely in treasury inventories. It is evident that for the greater part *Opus Tentonicum* derived its inspiration from contemporary paintings and even sculpture, works of art which, in turn, derived their inspiration from the artists of the East. Oriental and Byzantine influences are freely apparent not only in style but in the fabrics used. Silk for instance became known in the western markets by way of merchants from the Near East. Rich silk fabrics, velvets and brocades served in central Europe to carry an abundance of embroidery, mainly in couched work and utilizing gold and silver thread. The princely and ecclesiastical courts of the time used these embroideries extravagantly in pompous ceremonial displays.

The Emperor Charlemagne (768–814) encouraged the arts in all their forms. Embroiderers received his direct blessing. His court set an example in the pursuit of this craft.

A cope presented by Charlemagne has been preserved at Metz cathedral. Embroidered on it are great eagles with outstretched wings, their claws being bitten by legendary creatures. Threads of yellow, blue and green are used for the representation.

So universal was the eagle motif in the embroideries of Charlemagne that they came to be known as *aquilata*. The eagle was the insignium of Charlemagne's western empire and it retained its favour as a heraldic device in subsequent dynasties.

The high standard of embroidered work achieved in Charlemagne's reign did not pass with his decease. It was preserved mainly through the skill of women. Judith, mother of Charles the Bald, embroidered a baptismal mantle for her godson King Harold of Denmark when he visited Ingelheim in 826. Jewels were set in the cloth amid the magnificent motifs. Queen Adélais, the wife of Hugh Capet (987–996), another efficient needlewoman, gave a richly embroidered cope to the church of St Martin at Tours. The front showed the Adoration of the Lamb and the back showed the Deity surrounded by cherubin and seraphin.

Famous among extant examples of *Opus Teutonicum* dating from the eleventh century is that known as the Hungarian Coronation Cope, said to have been presented by St Stephen I of Hungary (997–1038) to the Church of St Mary at Szekesfehervar. The wife of Stephen, Queen Gisela, was a sister of the Emperor Henry II. She was skilful with her needle and encouraged the craft by setting up, near the palace, workshops for embroideresses. Tradition has it that in these workrooms originated *point de Hongrie* (Hungarian stitch) a name current at the present and indicating a specific stitch producing a zig-zag line.

Queen Gisela is reputed to have worked on the celebrated cope. The garment is made of crimson satin and is shot with shadings of blue and of gold. The embroidery on its lower edge shows a tree with symmetrical branches and confronting birds. Other groups surround it, the whole being assembled in lozenge diapering. Down the front and the back, a band of purple silk extends. The front bears a representation of Christ worked in gold. His right hand is raised in blessing and his left hand holds the Gospels. Below him is portrayed St Paul and above is St Peter. On the back panel, figures of the Apostles have been embroidered and the shoulder saddle bears the inscription *S. Hungarium R. et Gilsa, Delecta Sibi Conjux; Mittunt Haec Munera* DNO: *Apostolico Johanne* – 'Stephen, King of Hungary and Gisela, his dear wife, send this present to the Apostolic Lord St John.'

This reference to Pope John XVIII (1003–1009) dates the vestment. The Hungarian origin of the work is evident in its style and motifs. There is an interesting blend of eastern and western influences. Oriental trends are manifest in the balanced arrangement of figures and their stance – that of facing towards the front. There are also a number of Byzantine motifs. The western influence is to be seen in the *manner* in which these motives are portrayed.

Another – and possibly an even more important – specimen of *Opus Teutonicum* is the cope of the Emperor Henry II (1002–1024). It is now preserved in the cathedral treasury at Bamberg. Embroidery, rich in colouring and composed mainly of couched work, is worked on a silk ground which has been more recently restored. The designs are arranged around a central square and enclosed in polygons and circles; they illustrate an early conception of the world. Here again there is a blending of western and eastern influences; the figures on the cope are western in form but are introduced in Byzantine technique and arrangement. There is little ambiguity concerning this cope for an inscription on it – the lettering is western – states that it was made for the imperial coronation at the request of Duke Ismael of Apulia. The Emperor later presented it to the cathedral.

Henry may have presented several such gifts to the cathedral. It is known that he presented a chasuble embroidered in gold much after the manner of tapestry weaving, for the border of the garment is still preserved in the Bavarian Museum at Munich. The influence of the East is direct not only in style but in the motifs.

A dalmatic (vestment) of the eleventh century preserved in the treasury of St Peter's at Rome is by tradition reputed to have belonged to Charlemagne. Scientific evidence confutes this belief but the garment does date from the eleventh century. It displays magnificent embroidery; on a groundwork of blue silk are scattered crosses worked in blue and in silver. The fashion for roundels is evident and these appear on the front and on the back, and enclose scenes from the life of Christ. Other figures are worked outside the roundels. On the shoulders are designs portraying the bread and wine. All the scenes and figures have a unifying theme – the Adoration of Christ Triumphant.

An illuminating description of this embroidered work comes from the pen of Lady Marian Alford.

'It is done chiefly in gold, the draperies in basket and laid stitch, flat, with finely drawn outlines in black silk. The hair, the shadowy part of the draperies and the clouds are worked in fine gold and silver thread with dark outlines.'

An inscription worked on the dalmatic is in Greek.

Returning to a survey of the embroideries of the time of Emperor Henry II, we find the celebrated German state chasuble known as the cloak of Queen Kunigunde, wife of the Emperor. Here also the arrangement shows a Byzantine trend and the motifs are enclosed in circles; traditional biblical scenes are embroidered on the garment.

Rich embroidery in coloured silks and in gold worked upon precious fabrics, after the manner described, increased in number as the Middle Ages advanced. Some were copies of the more sumptuous garments of other countries; many were direct examples of *Opus Teutonicum*.

Even at this early stage it is just to acknowledge the existence of much simpler work which owed practically nothing to foreign influence. Simple materials and a simple technique characterized this indigenous work from which German embroidery was derived. This simple interpretation was evident in all those countries into which Teutonic influence penetrated. The embroiderers worked on linen in silk and in wool. They did not strive after the ambitious compositions usual among highly-skilled workers but portrayed dramatic scenes simply, achieving an indisputable richness of effect on their loosely-woven fabrics by the introduction of harmonious colours and brilliant silks.

Vestments representative of such work are to be seen in the monastery of St Blaise in the Black Forest of Austria. A cope of this work dating from the thirteenth century preserved in the Vienna Art Museum shows scenes from the life of Christ and from that of St Nicholas. A collection of four vestments and an antependium dating from the late thirteenth century preserved in the Museum of Art and Industry at Vienna shows embroideries of an obsolete kind. They are said to be the work of the nuns of Goess in Styria who were guided in their devotional task by the Abbess Kunigunde. The religious scenes are represented crudely and are flanked by formal conventionalized motifs. Some of the figures are well-proportioned and show artistry in skill and execution; others are crude in the extreme. A number of animals are portrayed which are all derived from mediaeval books on animals. Geometrical motifs completely fill the background. This juxtaposition of crude and skilled designs is inharmonious but the defects are blurred to some degree by the highly-skilled work displayed and the wide range of stitchery. The influence of the East is present in the introduction of scrolls, interlacing ribbons, squares and diamonds, features which established a secure place for themselves in German indigenous art.

As this primitive treatment became more widely known in northern Germany, its interpretation tended to become yet more archaic. Later it became an entity in itself having no powerful influence on subsequent work. Numerous specimens of fourteenth and fifteenth century work are to be seen in collections at Hanover, Halberstadt, Erfurt, Brunswick, Ebstorf and Lower Saxony. Convent work in Lower Saxony tended to show a certain lifeless uniformity in the later Middle Ages.

The specimens which have been retrieved from southern Germany are fewer in number although the craft of embroidery may have had a wide appeal there. An antependium from southern Germany is at the Historical Museum at Berne. This was presented by the Duke Albrecht II of Austria to the Abbess Adelheid for the service of the convent at

Koenigsfelden. French treatment of the subject matter is apparent for the scenes in the life of Christ are shown with the figures being embroidered in silk on a gold ground. The counts of Bohemia showed a predilection for this type of French work in their heraldic crests.

Linen embroidery, in which the weaving combined with the applied ornamentation, was much favoured in Germany. Gradually it came to be termed *Opus Coloniensis* or Cologne work. Flat diaper patterns in white and in coloured thread contributed to the total effect. The weavers employed low warp frames while shuttles carrying coloured threads were passed through the warp. The work was popular and specimens are numerous. Many are to be seen in the Victoria and Albert Museum. The distribution of the woven embroideries was wide even at the time of their manufacture. They were worked in the seclusion of castles, convents and monasteries but as some were made for sale they were displayed in the international fairs of Europe. In contrast to the linen woven on the low warp frames were the materials woven on high warp looms. These were used as bands or orphreys for copes. The Rhineland was a special centre for this work and the craft flourished there to a marked degree until the Renaissance.

Among the more remarkable specimens of German embroidery of the fourteenth century is an altar frontal from Sarnen kept in the Kunst-Gewerbe Museum at St Gallen. Although in a poor state of preservation, the remnants are sufficient to reveal the high standard and interest of the embroidery. Another attractive embroidery of this period is a linen cloth kept in the convent of Wienhausen. The fabric is made of coarse linen thread and the embroidery is in coloured silk. Flat stitch is employed for the greater part while sections show a basket weave formed by canvas stitches. The outlines are emphasized by darker silks. There are fifteen panels in all and these depict scenes in the childhood of Christ. An embroidered cloth in the monastery of Sion in the Swiss canton of Valais probably dates from the fourteenth century also. The cloth is of linen and the border is in red silk and gold thread. Another cloth, probably an altar cloth, is in the Cluny Museum in Paris; the embroidery is arranged in rows and takes the form of appliqué work. The biblical subjects are difficult to recognize today as the cloth is very worn. An altar cloth embroidered in Cologne work is in the Victoria and Albert Museum and is a particularly interesting example with figures woven into the fabric and details emphasized by thread. The figure of the Virgin Mary is accompanied by the words *Ave Maria*.

In the fifteenth century, German interest in wool embroidery was foremost. Designs were heterogeneous, many of them being inspired by the woodcuts of the time. Conventional foliage surrounded or screened profane mythological or biblical scenes. The main purpose of the woollen worsted embroideries was to serve as furnishing fabrics and for this reason they bore a close affinity to the tapestries of the time. Those woven cloths were made on a spectacular scale to cover bare walls and to exclude draughts and this purpose was also kept in mind while making wool embroideries. Designs were usually pictorial and they were worked out with astonishing detail. A considerable number of the large scale embroideries have survived but more numerous are long narrow bands which were made to cover the backs of wooden benches, chairs and pews. Pictorial designs are shown on them in a horizontal arrangement.

Fine linen was seldom used for the ground as coarse linen canvas was a more suitable vehicle for the woollen embroidery which was done for the greater part in convent stitch. The worsted thread was obtained from sheep's wool which had very little twist so these threads were secured with small overstitches of the same wool. The couching threads were placed closely together and as the wool was of a fleecy texture, the ground material was completely covered. The designs favoured were biblical scenes, lives of the saints, legends and armorial designs.

The woollen embroideries of Wienhausen and Lüneberg were particularly famous. The famous Tristram embroidery of the fifteenth century is in blue, red, yellow and green, the colours favoured in these hangings. This story of Tristram was a favourite one and embroiderers interpreted it according to local versions; the famous woollen embroidery depicts different scenes and the figures are clothed in the costumes of the time. The stitch used in the main is the Kloster stitch and is worked with an eye to economy.

Specimens of Lüneberg work show a resemblance of treatment to those worked in Wienhausen. The scenes favoured were biblical and as they carry inscriptions and dates their source is revealed to subsequent ages. The similarity in the designs is occasioned largely by the custom of copying designs issued by the convents. Many of the designs were made by the monks; some were created by laymen and were purchased by the embroiderers. There appears to have been a traditional custom governing the use of colours: borders were worked with a green ground and blue was used for the main ground. The Lüneberg embroideries have a more direct appeal than those of Wienhausen, the latter have to resort to lettering and inscriptions as an explanation of the story. It must be remembered that the embroideries were worked before printed books were used which explains the appeal of the embroideries at the time of their working and the lack of printed books accounts for the localized versions of general European stories.

Notable among the embroidery specimens made in southern Germany in the fourteenth century were the Malterer tapestries preserved in Freiburg and the tapestries preserved in the city hall at Ratisbon. Switzerland produced excellent work of high artistic design and advanced technical skill. The famous needle tapestry from Bischofzell is preserved in the Historical Museum at Basle and serves as a social document of real worth as it is a coloured representation of daily life in a small town. At the Basle museum there are also interesting genealogical needle tapestries and a wool tapestry at Zurich has as its subject a theme popular in the Middle Ages – *Weiberlisten* – 'Woman's Wiles'. In fact the work dates from the Renaissance period as it was worked in the sixteenth century but the general treatment of the embroidery and the framework of Gothic foliage links it more closely with work of the Middle Ages.

These woollen embroideries of Germany are unique and of an excellence greater than those produced in England, where embroiderers delighted to work in wool on linen but where work of this nature was on a smaller scale. German work had a distinctive freshness and fine workmanship and colours contributed happily to the narrative scenes.

In the fifteenth and sixteenth centuries German embroiderers favoured coloured linen thread (plate 46). Stitches were simple and formed diaper patterns emphasized with outline stitches; small quantities of gold thread being introduced when more magnificent effects were sought. It became evident at this stage that the embroiderers were emulating workers in needlepoint lace, a form of ornamentation enjoying a great vogue at the time. Some of the stitches resembled the *punto in aria* of the Italian workers but more generally a looped or chain stitch was used.

An excellent collection of this type of work is to be seen in the Historical Museum at St Gallen. Typical of the designs favoured are those shown on a set of biblical panels representing women of the Bible. A Nativity panel dated 1551 is in the Victoria and Albert Museum together with one dated 1584 showing an intriguing and amusing representation of the Marriage at Cana.

The seventeenth century witnessed the creation of more magnificent embroideries following on the development of textiles. Silk workers and weavers found refuge in Germany following on the Revocation of the Edict of Nantes and the immediate reaction was to ornament the magnificent materials created rather than allow them to be displayed in their own splendour.

Beadwork was a distinctive feature of seventeenth-century embroidery and the glass industries of Germany produced them in large quantities. Their use was not an innovation, however, for beads had been used lavishly on mediaeval vestments. The remains of a stole of German work dating from the thirteenth century and displaying beads of glass, coral and seed pearls can be seen in the Victoria and Albert Museum.

Oriental influences penetrated into Germany as elsewhere; Chinese and Indian embroideries were copied diligently when these fabrics were distributed into western Europe by the great trading companies. Embroiderers showed a preference for oriental pictorial subjects and worked them in coloured silks in chain stitch. The influence of the East increased in the following century and it is significant that the countries of western Europe sent fabrics to India and China to be embroidered by native embroiderers (plate 48).

In the nineteenth century, Germany was caught up in the race to facilitate sewing by mechanical means. Hand embroidery persisted however and Germany was the original source of a form of embroidery which was practised lavishly in most European countries viz. Berlin wool work. In 1810, a print seller of that city issued a number of needlecraft patterns; the venture proved an instant success. The stitchery was in Berlin wool dyed in the raw basic colours achieved by the newly-discovered aniline dyes and the work was ornamented further with beads.

This wool work was used for all manner of domestic furnishings as well as needlework pictures. Soft canvas formed the ground fabric of the stitchery and this was attached to a cloth ground. When the stitched work was complete the canvas threads were cut off. The soft fleecy wool came from flocks reared in Saxony and so great was the demand for the wool in embroidery that the wool trade of this district flourished and sheep breeders in England, Spain and France began to rear sheep of the Saxony breed.

Berlin work became a craze in America, supplanting much of the finer and more excellent work made there. Germany, however, fostered fine embroidery in the United States for, in the eighteenth century, the Sisters of Moravia established a school of needlework in Pennsylvania. It was through this school at Bethlehem that many in the New World became acquainted with or skilled in European forms of embroidery in all its many expressions. Domestic needlework of a high standard had become traditional since the settlement of the early colonists. Since the women of a later age were not called upon to live lives of daily toil, the eighteenth century was characterized by much exquisite embroidered work. (See page 142 ff.)

Germany became design conscious in the nineteenth century and a School of Needlework established in Crefeld influenced German needlecraft much after the manner of the Royal School of Needlework in England. In the face of machine-made textiles the embroiderer of today persists happily in interpreting present day designs as a sound expression of modern thought.

7 Swiss linen embroidery

Swiss linen embroidery is a term applied to a special class of work. It achieved its zenith in Switzerland and in certain provinces of Germany during the period extending between the early thirteenth century and the middle of the seventeenth century.

This work had a direct and naive appeal; it was not an aristocratic art nor did it in any way attempt to compete with the ambitious needle paintings produced at the same period in Italy, Flanders and England. Nevertheless, the Swiss linen work was based on a tradition of artistic merit although it was largely a direct expression of peasant life. Swiss mediaeval workers had already set a national standard of pictorial excellence in the tapestries which they wove during the Middle Ages. But linen work was a more natural medium to Swiss workers for silk embroidery was never an established craft there. Nevertheless, when the skill and artistic taste of the Swiss embroiderers was recognized internationally, they were not called upon to work on any spectacular cloths or rich garments.

The term Swiss work was a comprehensive one and served as the connotation for much embroidery worked in southern Germany. Inventories show clearly that much of the embroidery called Swiss work was created in Alsace. Today it is difficult to trace the exact locale of those specimens which have survived; characteristics and certain features of particular designs, such as those that appear on heraldic arms, offer some indication but this is not conclusive for the embroidery may well have been worked in other areas. Furthermore, the union of coats of arms by marriage complicates the evidence as regards the exact source of much of the work. Examples that have survived bear coats of arms referring to Lucerne, Baden, Zurich, Schaffhausen.

The French cantons of Switzerland were less attracted to linen embroidery than the German-speaking areas and most specimens appear to have been worked in those districts where linen was produced, namely St Gall, Constance, Appenzell and Schaffhausen.

The linen was of blue or brown yarn until the middle of the seventeenth century. The linen foundation contributed to the total effect for the ground was never covered over with the stitches which were usually worked in white thread. Although most of the work was done on unbleached linen, this is not evident on an examination of the specimens at the present time, for the cloths have been subject to frequent washing and to drying in the sun. Textile ingenuity is displayed in some of the older linens where the warp is composed of white flax whereas the weft is of cotton in a reddish brown colour achieved through the application of iron salts.

The width of the linen was governed by the small looms and this explains the narrow strips of about twenty-five inches in length which had to be secured together when a wide cloth was needed. Embroiderers showed themselves resourceful in securing these strips. Ornamental overstitching was sometimes used or embroidered braid or lace insertions were used to link the narrow bands.

Not only was the groundwork made of mixed materials but linens of different textures were used, particularly on pictorial designs. Coloured silk was introduced to mark features and in the earlier specimens it was used to emphasize outlines. This, in turn, emphasized the similarity between the designs and the woodcuts which inspired so many of them. Much of the coloured silk work has perished and but faint traces of it are apparent today.

Workers in coloured silks selected from a wide range of colours but linen yarns were restricted to white, brown, blue and yellow. Most work was done in white and in brown. Blue thread has faded with time and the brown has perished owing to the action of iron salts.

The stitches used were varied due to the characteristics of linen work in which every stitch appeared prominently. Each unit of a design demanded different treatment and varieties of particular stitches were also employed in one particular piece. Fortunately, the workers were familiar with a wide range of stitches for these had been in use since the thirteenth century. Technical excellency rather than variety characterized the work of the fourteenth and fifteenth century but in the following periods, under the influence of the Swiss workers, there was an efflorescence of varieties of dot stitches, stem stitches and outline stitches.

Much of the earlier work has been condemned on the ground that the standard of work was low and the taste execrable. A careful examination of early specimens is sufficient to show that such accusations are not unfounded. The stitches were irregular so that there is a general impression of untidiness, and the reverse side of the embroideries reveals negligent workmanship. In defence of the early specimens, however, there is an unmistakeable spontaneity and freshness which is wanting in many specimens of more accurate workmanship.

The Swiss peasant used whatever materials were at hand and created from them linen articles for daily use. In the mediaeval home, in particular, linen played an important part. Consequently, Swiss linen embroidery was used for far less ornate articles than those which called for silk embroidery. It is fortunate that specimens of this type of work are numerous. Moreover, old inventories make frequent reference to these embroideries but comments in these indicate that the Swiss embroideries, however well worked, were not regarded as being of any great value. An ecclesiastical inventory at Alsace refers collectively to certain embroideries as 'linen baggage... as to some of which it could not be determined to what use it was meant to be put'. The designs on the cloths give indication whether they were meant for ecclesiastical or lay use. Cloths were usually rectangular though round cloths were not unknown. Linen curtains and wall coverings or hangings were numerous as also were hand towels. Church furnishings included antependia fitted with removable borders and also hangings for pulpit desks and lecterns.

One of the earliest specimens of Swiss embroidery extant is a tablecloth believed to have been worked in the thirteenth century. It was formed of linen strips which were interlaced and the oval designs on it are fore-runners of medallions which were to prove popular in the succeeding era. A tablecloth of the fourteenth century is to be seen at the Historical Museum at Basle. It is a product of the Feldbach nunnery in Thurgovia and shows a design worked in white linen yarn and coloured silks depicting fabulous people and animals surrounded by circles. These designs were usual in the Swiss art of the period. The work has been done in the main in satin stitch together with a variety of lace stitches.

The Swiss National Museum at Zurich has a Swiss embroidery dating from the earlier half of the thirteenth century. The lettering of an inscription is of the period and reads 'He who strives for honour must bear God in mind and nothing will go wrong'. A border of pigeons encloses designs showing animals and naturalistic plants and these are linked together with scrolls. Plant ornaments were prominent in all Swiss embroideries and were never made subservient to geometric designs. As embroiderers grew more ambitious, flowers and fruits would be shown growing on the same branch. Interlacing scrolls were also much in evidence serving as useful filling-in designs in their spiral form or in a more Gothic form with ubiquitous tendrils. These scrolls and garlands seldom served as motifs in themselves; they were mainly used along with other foliage to set off the figures.

Gothic characteristics were apparent in Swiss work as late as the seventeenth century. When other European countries were experiencing the blossoming of Renaissance ideas Swiss designers were still clinging tenaciously to the mysticism of the Middle Ages, interpreting spiritual values of biblical scenes and pictorial designs which drew their inspiration from classical mythology and the mediaeval romances and epics. The symbolic value of the motifs was emphasized but little consideration was given to appropriate use. The embroideries never achieved a specific symbolism or iconography such as was attained by the more magnificent fabrics of Italy and Flanders. The designs of the Swiss workers of the later Middle Ages were not inspired by artists but by crude patterns which could be assimilated easily.

Biblical scenes predominated with scenes from the life of Christ being the most popular although crucifixion scenes are, however, far less frequent than in the embroideries of France, Italy, Flanders and England. Strange anachronisms appear in many of the scenes and figures from the Old Testament intermingle with those from the New. Furthermore, saints of post-biblical times are inserted and even secular subjects appear in the midst of the prophets and apostles.

The symbolism of the mediaeval ages was apparent in Swiss linen embroidery; the Lamb of God for instance was represented with a halo and a flag. The four evangelists were introduced into embroideries for pictorial purposes for they also formed a convenient set for filling the corners of a rectangular cloth. Symbolic animals appear frequently though the degree of symbolism may be open to question. It is improbable that the embroiderers were influenced either directly or indirectly by the *Physiologus*. This bestiary which probably had its source in Alexandria was one of the mediaeval books which gave descriptions of animals and which interpreted these animals allegorically as types of the spiritual life. Such books were popular for they promulgated the allegorizing tendencies of the early Christians. The *Physiologus* was translated into many languages and it appealed to a wide public. Motifs illustrated in it were used extensively in all forms of mediaeval art: the phoenix was interpreted as a symbol of eternal life in that it rose from its own ashes; the lion was a symbol of the resurrection; the pelican, cutting itself open to feed its young, was recognized as a symbol of the crucifixion and the unicorn stood for the Virgin Mary. A mediaeval legend of Indian origin, which was then later dispersed in Europe by way of Mesopotamia, maintained that this fabulous animal could only be caught by a virgin, thus the unicorn hunt was interpreted in embroidery by a representation of the Archangel Gabriel accompanied by hounds on a leash (these being representative of the Christian virtues) driving a unicorn towards the Virgin Mary.

The linen embroidery of the mediaeval period was not, however, a vehicle for the direct interpretation of symbolic motifs; secular themes were interspersed and among the scrolls and banderols lovers were shown, often accompanied with inscriptions of faith and of love. Insincerity in love was an ever recurring theme, such as that in embroideries showing a woman weighing a heart against a feather. Women's wiles – the *Weiberlisten* – were a constant figural subject.

The scenes seldom cover the whole groundwork. Figures and landscapes were arranged artistically and set within wreaths or medallions and there was a tendency to link and interlace such circles, a practice which had been favoured by the mosaic workers of Rome and the tapestry workers of the Hellenistic world.

A white linen embroidery of Swiss work formed an important item in the Figdor Collection in Vienna before its transference to Berlin. Basle is probably the place of origin. The designs show two lovers beside a tree and ribbons and leaves screen the happy pair. The cloth was originally intended as a wall hanging.

A table runner in the Historical Museum at Berne is worked in brown and linen yarn and shows scenes illustrating the theme of *Weiberlisten*. The scenes are arranged on opposite sides of the cloth and they show strong men becoming the dupes of artful women. Samson is shown with Delilah, Holofernes with Judith, Aristotle with Phyllis, Virgil with the daughter of the Emperor. The central motif shows the arms of Hans Lyb of Schaffhausen and Anna Messnang of Constance. The crest bears the date 1510 but there is evidence that this date was added at a later period. The style of work and the stitchery suggest that the cloth was worked in the previous century.

The transition period, culminating in the Renaissance, produced a medley of motifs. This confusion showed the struggle between the Gothic and Renaissance ideas. But, gradually, late Gothic scrolls, garlands and letterings gave way to the more orderly and balanced arrangements of Renaissance interpretation.

During the sixteenth century, embroiderers turned frequently to the popular illustrated books of the time. Woodcuts were studied carefully. Bible woodcuts took precendence. It was fortunate that the woodcuts of the period were produced by competent artists such as Hans Holbein the Younger, Beham, Virgil Solis and Stummer. Workers in stained glass were dependent on special models for their figural scenes but embroiderers were well content to study the illustrations in woodcuts.

Characteristic of the work of the second half of the sixteenth century is a linen wall hanging preserved in the Historical Museum at Basle. Inscribed with the date 1563, it shows a scene from the legend of Tobias and derives its inspiration from work of Hans Holbein the Younger in the Froschauer Bible of 1540. In the Bible, the scene has a rectangular setting but the embroiderer has enclosed it within a medallion of foliage. Differences between the two scenes were inevitable due to the different media in which the artists worked. Grace of line was sacrificed in needlework but there was full compensation in the needle's ability to interpret and enhance flat surfaces.

The Renaissance motifs, such as that of the vase, were adopted very slowly in Swiss linen work for the embroiderers were conservative in their tastes. Certain forms such as architectural scroll work were eschewed and later baroque motifs were also debarred in the linen medium. New motifs, when they were accepted, soon became hackneyed for embroiderers resorted to the pattern books published in the sixteenth and seventeenth centuries. Embroidery by now was regarded as a feminine craft and the inscription of *The New Modelbuch* published at St Gall in 1593 is dedicated – 'To all virtuous women and damsels, needleworkers; likewise to any other desirous to undertake such artistic work'. Samplers were also models for linen embroiderers and although it is possible that artists contributed designs there is no direct evidence of this beyond the accuracy and skill apparent in much of the work. Significant too is a passage in a letter written in 1575 to Frau Veritas and Jungfrau Dorothea Bullinger of Zurich by Frau Ursula Marschelkin of Baffenheim. 'I have always had in mind the model sketch for the table cover; but I have not been able to get the painter – because he is not at home – to sketch it, so that it cannot be as yet. But as soon as it is painted, I shall ask you to take it in hand.'

The Swiss linen embroideries of the late sixteenth and early seventeenth century are numerous but it is not easy to place them chronologically for Gothic motifs still linger among Renaissance designs. Typical of Renaissance work is a linen panel dated 1544 bearing the arms of the Dorer family of Baden. The inscription reads 'Heinrich Dorer and Margaret Orli by Konrad Dorer (and) Madalena Dorer 1544.'

Mediaeval influences penetrated into the Renaissance work known as the *Hortus Conclusus* antependium kept in the Swiss National Museum in Zurich. Symbols of the Virgin Mary and in particular the Mystic Garden of Mary were ever popular motifs.

The designs and workmanship of Swiss linen embroidery had their main source of inspiration in the Catholic Church. It was not an outcome of peasant art although expressions of this, based on designs evolved from the right angles formed by warp and weft, found their place in this particular type of work. Stars and rosettes, wheels and stylized flowers assumed, however, a subordinate place. Nevertheless peasant interpretation of the embroideries is all-important for this above all accounts for the charm and individuality of the work. M. Daniel Baud-Bovy in his *Peasant Art in Switzerland* has assessed its worth accurately; he maintains that the 'women weavers... and the rustic embroideresses who are the real originators and often without consciously innovating, lend something of their own individuality to the decoration... to the patterns handed down from generation to generation; to the samplers taught at school; a something which is infused into the work, as it springs into being under their fingers, a full-blooded warmth, akin to that of Nature's sap. We have seen the peasant women of the Lötoschenthal engaged in embroidering, without patterns, designs for bodice sleeves and collars for habit-shirts – designs closely related to the carved decorations of chalets while the Grisons' embroideries on baptismal robes or on the coverings of children's cots in time of mourning, represent one of the most widespread and original sources of our rustic art.'

8 Italy

Opus Italicum

The partly-civilized races who overthrew the Roman Empire were concerned with the necessities of life, caring nothing for the refining graces of civilized ways of living. Centuries of darkness engulfed Europe but the longest night is followed by day and here the dawning came in benighted Italy.

As the cities of the peninsula grew great and independent, they developed commercially. The merchant princes opened up trade routes to India by way of Constantinople, Trebizond and Persia. For several centuries, the main cities of Italy became the chief marts and distributing centres between the semi-civilized nations of western Europe and the age-long civilizations of the East, inhabited as those regions were by enervated peoples.

Italy and Spain were to benefit directly from eastern influences during the Middle Ages. The Sicilian textile industry flourished because the Saracens taught the art of weaving in silk and in gold cloth and royal patronage was bestowed on these crafts. When King Robert II returned from a Grecian expedition in 1145, he introduced weavers from Argos and Corinth into Sicily. The textile workshops of Palermo flourished and Sicily soon attained an international reputation for her silk fabrics, her velvets and her brocades. Allied to this skill in weaving was that of embroidery and coverings for tables, doors and floors were made with designs worked in coloured threads. A technique which enjoyed a great vogue was that which called for the use of two fabrics; the pattern was cut in one and stitched on to the other with overstitching in polychrome silks. These were referred to as Saracenic cut cloths.

The cities of the mainland soon benefited from Sicilian advance. Craftsmanship was always honoured in Italy where it was given special recognition as the handmaid of the Roman Catholic Church. The textiles and ornamented fabrics of Italy contributed to her wealth and the great seaports benefited from trade in them. Unfortunately, these great seaports, following on early development and great commercial expansion, then diverted their energies to mutual destruction and consequently all forms of artistic expression suffered adverse effects. The popes, constant benefactors of the crafts, took advantage of the weakness of the Empire and consolidated the papal states. But by the fifteenth century, Italy was, however, settling down once again to a more tranquil condition and the minute factions into which she was divided up consolidated roughly into five larger states. The rulers of these, once their position was secure, adopted humane and enlightened policies and their subjects enjoyed a great measure of prosperity. Consequently the fifteenth century was a time of great commercial advance and in this area of southern Europe were first seen the beginnings of the great intellectual and artistic movement known as the Renaissance. Outstanding among the aristocratic families of Italy in this century were the Medicis who, if they demoralized Florence by luxury, gave her peace and prosperity. It was due to their encouragement of the arts that Florence was kept in the forefront in the world of culture.

The influence of the Medicis on the French arts was also profound. Members of the Medici family lived in luxury and portraits of them indicate, among other things, their love of embroidery. Lorenzo de' Medici (1448–92), known as the Magnificent, was one of the most distinguished scholars of his age and was well versed in every branch of art and science. His portrait by Benozzo Gozzoli in the Riccardi Palace at Florence, shows him wearing a suit embroidered richly in coloured silks and spangles.

Designs favoured in the Middle Ages were in the main religious and heraldic and were characterized by a style that one may term militant. Life was warfare to the mediaeval craftsman and this philosophy expressed itself in the patterns he created. The technique of embroidered work shows a refinement of taste which was unfortunately lost in a later age which sought after more sumptuous and dazzling effects. Oriental and Byzantine influences were pronounced and were adopted with zeal as they gave the pattern maker and the embroiderers an opportunity for varied ornamentation in their work. Greater variety of expression and of execution became apparent as time went on but throughout the Middle Ages there was maintained a common denominator of frankness and a pleasing boldness of expression.

Linen work was favoured, in particular, in Italy where it was soon to develop into a fine art as needlepoint lace. Interest in linen work embroidery captivated the whole of central Europe and this form of expression has retained its vogue throughout the centuries. Much of the Italian linen work of the period resembles that on the Lüneberg embroideries. Infinite care and diligence were spent on linen embroidery work and much of it was in 'open work'. A thread was wrapped around two or three threads of the material for certain units of the design where sometimes soft yellow or blue silks were introduced into the work along with the linen thread. Outlines were often worked in chain stitch while flesh was represented by means of flat stitches introduced obliquely. Groundworks often showed diaper patterns which covered the foundation of the design and gave an effect of weaving.

Some first-rate specimens of fifteenth century Italian linen work are kept in the Kunst-Gewerbe Museum, St Gallen. Some short borders representing hunting scenes were often done in attractive combinations of colours: men and women were shown in contemporary costumes which were coloured blue and brown; beasts were represented in light brown and landscapes were treated realistically. Other borders, showing a more ecclesiastical bias, showed motifs such as crosses and palmettes interspersed between symbolic lambs and lions. Symbolic beasts also appeared on heraldic designs and lions, unicorns and eagles featured among the beasts. Gold and metal threads were sometimes used on motifs and grounds were sprinkled with spangles, each spangle being held in position by a single stitch.

Certain of the medallions on orphreys (bands of gold embroidery) which have perished, have survived to the present day. Among these is a medallion in the Carmichael Collection, the design of which is attributed to a Florentine painter of repute, Antonio Pollaiuolo (1433–98). The figures show the Virgin Mary and the Infant Christ greeted by St Donatus. Much of the work is done in couching, the gold threads being laid on in pairs. While sections of the design are padded, silk stitching served to represent the flatter surfaces and gold thread introduced light. Pearls were originally inserted into the crowns.

The specimens of Italian linen work that date from the sixteenth century reveal that great advance was made in fabrics with open texture ornamented with solid embroideries.

Threads were drawn from the linen so that the remaining fabric resembled fine gauze and with the aid of a coarse linen thread, the embroiderer darned a pattern on the threads. With remarkable ingenuity figures – often biblical – were darned together with their accompanying emblems. Much of the work was in the form of borders taking narrative themes as subjects of design; and was characterized by uniformity, evenness and a certain freedom of expression. The technique used in tapestry weaving was used in this darned work which was often referred to as *lacis* or net work; but strictly speaking, the *lacis* or net work of Italy referred to a form of needlework of a special kind entirely different in technique from the darned work. In *lacis* proper the threads were not removed from the fabric; instead, on a groundwork of loosely woven linen, groups of threads were caught together by overcast threads drawn tightly leaving an openwork area in the foundation cloth. The two types of darned work were sometimes introduced into the same piece of work with pleasing effect. The Victoria and Albert Museum possesses specimens of such work, known as Italian linen work, which have a foundation of brown threads while the stitches are worked in white.

In the sixteenth century, Italy was the chief country disseminating its designs throughout Europe through the medium of pattern books on embroidery and on laces. Moreover it was to Italy that many embroiderers turned for their materials: the Milanese supplied needles, Lucca provided gold threads and Sicily and Lombardy, by means of their silkworms, fostered the manufacture of silk in Europe.

The interest in culture fostered by the mediaeval popes and nobles was continued under their Renaissance successors (plate 54). Pope Julius II, Pope Leo X de' Medici and Pope Paul III dei Farnese each in turn encouraged artists and craftsmen and the papal policy was then echoed by that of the dukes of Milan, Florence and Ferrara and the doges of Venice. Italian embroiderers achieved an even greater international reputation. Specimens of Italian work were among the most treasured possessions of every country in Europe, valuable in themselves and as sources of inspiration for other embroiderers.

Italian embroidery of the sixteenth century reveals the fact that the workers showed meticulous care in the working of the smallest details. Inspired by the subtle tones and shadings of Italian paintings, the embroiderers introduced gradations of shade into their work and made a deliberate study of the blending of colours. So eager were the embroiderers to achieve an effect similar to that produced by painters, that, at times, they borrowed the painter's brush and expressed flesh tints by painting. This exaggeration of sheer technique was not commendable though it was a practice imitated readily by the embroiderers of other countries in this and in succeeding centuries.

This mixing of materials seemed to have appealed strongly to Italian embroiderers. Venetian workers, for instance, resorted to the use of the glass beads manufactured in their city and reverted to work reminiscent of that of the early Egyptians. Such work, specimens of which can be seen at the Victoria and Albert Museum, has very little fascination today, although the frankness of the design and gaiety of expression may have some appeal. Such beadwork had very little utilitarian value for it created a hard, unyielding surface, unsuitable for furnishing or costume save in small areas of the fabric. Beadwork wore badly, for apart from making the material heavy, it also required delicate handling as each bead hung upon a single thread.

Italian artists created designs for embroiderers revealing once again the close unity of the crafts prior to the coming of the machine age. Indeed first-rate artists eagerly accepted commissions to design work for embroiderers. An instance of this – and also of direct papal patronage – lies in the fact that Pierino del Vaga (1500–47) was commissioned by Pope Paul VIII to make a series of eight drawings illustrating incidents in the life of St Peter, in order that embroiderers could work the designs on a cope. Raphael, Cosimo Tura, Ercole Grandi and Dosso Dossi also prepared designs for embroiderers.

Certain of the Italian embroideries in the Kunst-Gewerbe Museum, St Gallen, suggest a masterly designer. Much of this work is on a drawn thread foundation with additional threads of silk introduced into the fabric. Several cloths are worked in red silk, the main stitch being back stitch. Outlines were emphasized by means of double running stitch.

Italian embroidery of the seventeenth century showed direct influence from the East. Special attention was given to furnishing materials and cushions were embroidered for painted and gilt furniture; large floral patterns were used and the work was done in floss silk. Embroiderers vied with each other in covering the whole surface of a fabric, whether embroidering materials for furnishing or for costume. Gold thread was laid with silks and used in basket stitch with gold wire. Gold lace was used extensively as a trimming.

Through her trading connections, Italy became acquainted at an early date with covering cloths that came from India, Persia and the Near East. The embroiderers made faithful replicas of the woven fabrics and advanced to an individual interpretation of eastern patterns.

Italian embroiderers used floss silks in conjunction with paper in the eighteenth century. This was recognized as a special kind of embroidery and was called *colifichet*. The technique was used in the creation of pictures which showed two surfaces simultaneously. The finished work was mounted between two sheets of glass. Smaller specimens of this work were used as bookmarkers in valuable books. Designs showing sacred subjects and flowers were often introduced into this type of work.

Embroidery forms an important feature of the peasant art of Italy. To those women living away from towns it was the chief form of aesthetic expression and weaving in flax, wool or in silk was a kindred occupation.

Embroidery designs were largely traditional for the workers had little ability in draughtsmanship and therefore copied closely those designs already known. As they counted the stitches and copied the designs, they were often ignorant of the fact that many of the patterns had originally been drawn by artists of repute in the fourteenth and fifteenth centuries. Abstract motifs and symbols had but little appeal and the peasant woman showed a preference for representations of living things well known to her in her daily life. A large number of the motifs were used widely in all parts of the peninsula.

Peasant workers showed a delight in using brightly coloured threads. Red predominated among others; the darker shades of red were used in the north whereas in the sunny south the more brilliant shades prevailed. Light and shade was introduced effectively but laws of perspective were ignored; for example, a child taller than a mountain would be represented guiding a stag bigger than both. Interpretations were often childish and were without rhyme or reason. A cow's horns stood several inches away from its head and a lamb would skip on the head of a lion; but the enthusiastic worker, revelling in her love of colour, was blind to the incongruities.

A girl was initiated into the craft of embroidery when young. She began at an early age to embroider a trousseau and in the meantime encouraged the favours of her swains by presenting them with handkerchiefs and scarves on which she embroidered love verses. She found the needle more to her purpose than the pen. Married women embroidered the clothes of their young children. Here again there was shown a delight in the embroidered word for baby clothes bore such expressions as *Cresci Santo* – Grow up Holy; *Gioia* – Joy; *Bello di Mamma* – Mother's Beauty. The aged women embroidered cloths for their burial, which included a shroud, a pillow case and head cloth. Peculiar to certain Italian districts were little grave flags bearing embroidered symbols and dirges.

A love of inscriptions may have been inspired by Roman Catholic ritual. The peasant women of the Marches, in direct contact with Papal rule, were prone to embroider articles in daily use. They forsook coarse linens and woollen fabrics and utilized fine materials on which they worked white stitches in a variety of forms. The workers used *punto reale* or royal stitch and *punto scritto*, stitches which ensured solid blocked surfaces.

Cross stitch or *punto in croce* was widely practised but was subject to varied interpretations. The wealthier regions of Italy delighting in magnificent effects, worked their cross stitches very finely in rich silks and gold and silver thread. Embroiderers of the Abruzzi worked their stitches in red cotton on coarse linens. The excellence of the work and the appropriateness of design concealed the poverty of the materials used.

In the rural districts bordering on Rome, peasant women embroidered the trappings of horses and of oxen. The wealth and social status of the owner were indicated by the rich embroideries which his animal bore. Coverings were sometimes embellished to the total exclusion of the groundwork. Frequently too, embroidery designs were limited to wide and rich borders which were enhanced with fringes. Predominating colours were red, blue, yellow and orange. Motifs were derived directly from the fields and included in the main flowers, birds and animals.

Peasant costumes afforded opportunities for embroidery work. The materials were rich in themselves, comprising brocades, cloth of gold, velvets and damasks. These were ornamented further with coloured stitchery. The origins of these peasant costumes, which in many cases are so alien to the practical rural way of life, have often been a subject of speculation. Do they represent an arrested advance of fashion, the residue of a richer age bequeathed to the poorer classes or are they the official uniforms bestowed by ancient lords on their vassals? It is a fascinating pursuit to observe how the practical peasant, ever waging a war of ways and means, adapted a costume intended for more luxurious wear to his own essential needs. Elaborate sleeves were made detachable in order to allow for greater freedom of movement and ornamented aprons were donned to save the richer garments from soiling. The peasant woman, ever practical, incorporated the use of a small stiff bodice and as this was worn constantly she economized on the strips of embroidery worked on her blouse, limiting it to those regions which were exposed when the bodice was worn.

Designs on these peasant costumes are simple. Lovers' mottoes are often worked on the garments. Heraldic symbols showing dragons, lions, gryphons, stags are worked in coloured thread. There is a strong predilection towards the use of figures. Pictorial scenes are much in evidence.

The charm of the specimens lies largely in the fact that they represent the embroiderer's individual taste both in technique and artistic representation. Despite foreign invasions and foreign influences, the embroideries remain pre-eminently expressions of Italian peasant craft.

9 *Spain and Portugal*

Nature has blessed the Iberian Peninsula with a lavish hand but much of its history has been darkened by bigotry, intolerance and oppression resulting from the administration of its lay and ecclesiastical rulers.

When the Roman legions withdrew from Spain the country was sub-divided into many small kingdoms each ruled by a petty king. Internal war was continuous and the Moors of northern Africa, watching their opportunity were able, with comparative ease, to over-run the more southerly regions of the country. In Spain, perhaps more than in other countries which they conquered, the Moors developed to a high degree arts and sciences and utilized them for the benefit of manufactures and of trade. In direct contrast to the warlike campaigns of the Moors were their successful projects in the arts of peace. The skill of their architectural work is evidenced in such buildings as the Alhambra. Their delight in decorative textiles was strong and their influence far exceeded those regions over which they held political power. The commercial-minded Moors sold their woven embroidered materials to neighbouring countries bordering the Mediterranean Sea and carried them far afield to Constantinople and to the great fairs of Europe. Here the sumptuous wares were bought eagerly and were valued both for their own intrinsic worth and as models for further craftsmanship.

The expulsion of the Moors from Spain in the sixteenth century led to their settlement in Algeria where they established a tradition in fine embroidery which was characterized by features peculiar to the region. Nevertheless certain features of colour, design, stitch and purpose were akin to those practised on the Iberian peninsula and hence are worthy of attention as being affiliated to the European tradition of embroidery. Algerian specimens of embroidery are confined in the main to curtains, head-shawls and kerchiefs. The curtains were hung before doors and were composed of three widths of linen joined together by an insertion usually of ribbon work. A long narrow width of linen was also embroidered as a head-scarf; part of it was sewn to form a hood and two long ends down each side made loose flaps-lappets. The head-kerchief had embroidered borders and a plain central piece. The work was done on loosely woven linen or cotton material and the stitches were in floss silk dyed with natural dyes, with the finer work being embroidered in red and blue. Later and coarser embroideries were in mauve. The older work was carried out in a characteristic brick stitch; later work showed a variety of stitches including a preponderance of eyelet holes and herringbone stitch.

Moorish influence in Spain had its roots in Persia. Persian architects were settled in Toledo and other towns conquered by the Saracens and Moors but it is probable that many other craftsmen were settled in the peninsula. Textile workers must have been among them and an Hotel de Tiraz was established in Almeira as well as in Sicily. It is significant that the word *tiraz* passed into the Spanish language as a generic name for ornamental fabrics.

Spanish art derived wealth also from the Incas of Peru who had achieved a high standard of culture and who have bequeathed to the modern world beautiful textiles adorned with embroideries which have never been rivalled. Peruvian patterns had a religious significance which was retained in part when they were interpreted by Spanish embroiderers. Human figures, birds (plate 58) and animals were symbolic as well as decorative.

Having inherited such a strong tradition of beautiful textiles it is not surprising to find that, in the Middle Ages, Spain had achieved a high standard in her production of textiles. Some of her finer fabrics were composed of velvet brocades on satin grounds interwoven with metallic threads. Gold and silver were introduced discreetly against a background of subdued colours. *Paillettes* were also introduced into dark fabrics and were set off with seed pearls. The inappropriateness of these ornamentations led to their early modification and soon little metal discs of gold and silver replaced them and although still inharmonious in texture, they were valued for their shining effects.

Spanish embroiderers showed a strong delight in the use of these spangles which they acknowledged as having a Saracenic origin. The uses to which they put them were often fortunate. One of the most remarkable examples of this spangled work is a chasuble reputed to be the work of Isabella la Catolica. It was taken by King Ferdinand to the cathedral at Granada in 1492 in the procession celebrating the taking of the town from the Moors.

Golden rings were introduced into some vestments instead of spangles and although they made the garments heavier, their effect on rich velvet grounds was magnificent.

The Moorish influences continued to prevail in Spain after the expulsion of the Moors and despite the growing use of Italian patterns. The influence of the Moriscos, as they came to be known in Christian Spain, prevailed in all forms of art in southern Europe and nowhere was it more pronounced than in embroidery. In 1609 under Philip III (1578–1621) there was a further expulsion of the Moriscos from Spain but their work was still in great demand in Spain and edicts were passed forbidding the importation of embroidery and lace into the peninsula.

Spanish work, a specific form of embroidery, enjoyed a great vogue in most European countries in the Renaissance period. In England it was connected with the coming of Catherine of Aragon. It is probable that this black-and-white outline embroidery derived its origin from Moorish work. Its lineage was yet older for the twined stitch was employed by primitive civilizations in the manipulation of fibrous textiles. As Spanish work evolved during the Renaissance, it took the form of all-over patterns making generous use of climbing stems and tendrils bearing fruit and flowers. The embroidery was worked in black silk on white linen with metallic threads introduced at times to add touches of glamour. The work was done in stem and back stitches, couching, knots and open chain.

Spanish influence continued to prevail in England under Mary Tudor on account of the nationality of her consort Philip II (1507–1598). There was also a preponderance of Spanish influence in France in the early seventeenth century following on the marriage of the Spanish princess, Anne of Austria, to Louis XIII. Among the beautiful embroideries which she took to France on the occasion of her marriage at the age of fourteen, Anne took an embroidered bedspread ornamented with eagles and crowns and bearing a rich border with motifs of animals, birds and flowers. Anne's influence was strong during the years of the minority of her son, Louis XIV.

Meanwhile at home Spanish embroiderers had been resourceful in building up a reputation of excellence (plate 57) in their craft. The standard of work rivalled closely that of Italy in design and artistic excellence. Much of the embroidery was inspired by

Spanish painters who derived their inspiration from the Italian schools and who were subject to the sombre restricting influence of the Spanish church and the Inquisition. The most pleasing of Spanish work was derived from the paintings of Murillo, whose gypsy settings were acceptable to the people. An embroidered picture inspired by him is in the Spitzer collection and shows the Holy Family in a rural setting. Other attractive needlework pictures of Spanish work, characterized by many of the features of oil paintings, are in the Cluny Museum, Paris.

Among the more spectacular of Spanish embroideries are altar cloths embroidered in gold thread worked effectively on grounds of rich red velvet. In the Spitzer collection is a lectern cover which, according to tradition, was given to the monastery of St Juste in Estremadura by Charles v when he entered into its seclusion in 1558. On a ground of red velvet flowers and S-motifs are worked in gold. Pictorial designs are shown on panels.

Another interesting specimen of Spanish work is a herald's tabard in the Archaeological Museum at Ghent. It dates from the late sixteenth century and was used when the Spanish Netherlands were ruled by Ferdinand and Isabella.

Much of the Spanish embroidery work was closely allied to what was termed 'passementerie', drawn work and lace. Motifs often reflected those commonly found in more openwork designs where the forms encroached on lace work. In drawn work which had an affinity with embroidery, colour was used sparingly, the embroiderers being content to work in black, blue and brown. White was sometimes introduced but more usually light effects were achieved by honey and cinnamon threads. In Castille much work was done in blue and honey coloured threads. This was used on towels and the term *toallas* was applied not only to the towels but to the particular kind of embroidered work.

This form of embroidery was used lavishly in the Renaissance period, the workers making designs of animals and utilizing geometric patterns on curtains, valances and bedspreads. The wheel and the sun motifs were traditional in Seville and these found popularity in the Spanish colonies. Embroidered work of this kind was used also on ecclesiastical and lay vestments.

Spanish embroiderers were skilled in ornamenting fine netting and cloths of delicate texture such as muslin. Andalusian workers had practised the decorating of network with embroidery stitches in the sixteenth century. Work was done not only on coarse nets but on those of fine silk bobbin texture. Similarly delicate work was done on fine muslin in the seventeenth century and this form of expression retained its popularity despite the influx of rich embroideries from the East. Favourite colours were black and white and black and red with touches of blue and of yellow.

The *muestrario* or sampler was a favourite form of Spanish work as were also the *abecedario* or embroidered alphabets. An inventory of Juana la Loca refers to as many as fifty samplers in the collection of the needleworker. The earliest samplers were long and narrow and were worked in linen and the stitches were mainly cross and flat stitches. Later samplers were oblong or square with the motifs worked in horizontal rows. Tassels were attached to corners and the edges were hem-stitched. The samplers of the eighteenth and nineteenth centuries had borders with a central panel displaying heterogeneous designs comprising geometrical and floral patterns. Stitches were more varied than in the earlier samplers and included in addition to the traditional cross and flat stitches variations of knot stitches, chain, feather, stem, coral, buttonhole and braid stitches.

Nowhere more than in Spain does embroidery reflect national vicissitudes. In 1492 the Moors were expelled from Spain where their rule, their civilization, their arts and their crafts had dominated for over seven hundred years. The loss to Spanish culture was made good by Columbus (1435–1506) who discovered the New World for Spain. Prosperity resulted from the conquest of American colonies and the wealth obtainable from her new resources was reflected in Spanish embroideries. The sixteenth century witnessed the zenith of Spanish glory. This was, however, short-lived and, under rasping rulers and an intolerant church, Spain entered on a long period of decadence in the seventeenth century – a decadence which expressed itself in all forms of her art.

In Portugal, embroidery was primarily an aristocratic craft practised assiduously by ladies with ample leisure and soft hands. Work was embroidered for secular and ecclesiastical purposes and in the main the characteristics of work done in Spain and the foreign influences which penetrated it affected Portugal also. There were certain inevitable differences however; Portugal was essentially a seafaring country and there was direct importation of eastern designs. Garments and church furnishings of the sixteenth century are fraught with Indian and Chinese designs with motifs of butterflies, dragons and exotic birds predominating (plate 58). A peculiar technique was practised, the embroiderers achieving an effect whereby the front of the embroidery was covered in silk while the reverse side showed the design in outline. Work was done in rich colourings achieved by natural dyes (plate 61), the colours of which were reminiscent of the richest work of painters in oils. Economy of the use of expensive materials was achieved by the application of stitches so that they appeared on the surface of the work and not on the reverse side.

Polychrome work was characteristic of Portugal as well as Spain, but white work was a favourite form in the more northerly districts where the work was particularly fine and made generous use of eyelet stitchery. On the other hard, the peasant embroideries (plate 62) of Portugal are very colourful and include stitches in red and black, pink and vivid green. These are worked on linen of a coarse texture and hand-woven. The patterns used were traditional and were based on geometric, plant and animal forms. Indigenous fruits and plants such as the vine, olive and orange were depicted amid conventional Renaissance motifs such as the vase or trophy.

10 *Flanders*

Flemish weavers were pre-eminent in the Middle Ages. They created rich brocades which rivalled those of Italy. Flanders and Burgundy were united under the same sovereign for so long a period that it is difficult at the present time to allocate the precise origin of certain fabrics. The woollen industry which provided the industrial power of the cities was introduced into the country by Baldwin III in the tenth century. England fed the Flemish looms with wool and woollen yarn.

The fabrics produced on these looms were highly decorative, many of them being inspired by French painters whose knowledge of the technical skill involved in the work reflects back to a time when craftsmanship had a more universal outlook and there was no social division separating one art from another.

The rich textiles manufactured were enhanced still further by embroidery (plate 63, 64). Here again designs were created by artists and the work supplied not only a local need but provided an important item in export trade. France, in particular, was a ready customer for Flemish decorative textiles. Designs on many French orphreys reveal a Flemish origin.

Examples of some of the earliest Flemish embroideries are to be seen at the Ambras College in Vienna. They form a set of sacerdotal robes and include two dalmatics, a chasuble, three copes and two antependia. The foundation is cloth of gold and the figures are embroidered in polychrome silks. The brilliant colourings were characteristic of the work done at the time. The designs were prepared by the brothers Van Eyck and their pupils. Not content with the richness of the textile materials, the embroiderers adorned the crowns and haloes of the saints with precious stones and many of the figures were outlined with pearls. The embroideries belong to the first half of the fifteenth century, if there is truth in the tradition that they were used at the first calling of the chapter of the Order of the Golden Fleece which took place on January 10th, 1430.

The influence of the painters of the Flemish and Dutch schools cannot be over estimated. All the arts flourished with the development and prosperity of the Low Countries. The Flemish Van Eycks were the great leaders and their discovery of the use of oil as a medium opened out possibilities of brilliant colouring which had their repercussions on embroideries. Italian influence later penetrated to textiles by way of painters and, when Spanish tyranny was relaxed, an indigenous Flemish school reached its finest expression with Rubens (1577–1640) and his pupils Van Dyck (1599–1641) and Teniers (1610–1690).

Flemish embroiderers are accredited with the creation of the magnificent embroideries belonging to Charles the Bold, son of Philip the Good. This Duke of Burgundy (1433–1477) is familiar to many through the fine delineation of him by Sir Walter Scott in *Quentin Durward*. Charles was defeated by the Swiss at Grandson on March 2nd 1476 and the embroideries formed part of the spoil. According to Philip de Commines, the Swiss 'seized his camp and cannon and all the tents and the pavilions belonging to him and his retinue which was very numerous and took possession of all the belongings of the said duke'.

It is fortunate that many of the fabrics including four hundred pieces of silk and tapestry were not distributed unwisely but were preserved in cathedral treasuries and later found a permanent home in museums and at the cathedral at Berne. The hat of Charles the Bold is among the most arresting of the specimens; it is of yellow velvet ornamented with a diamond aigrette and pearls and plumes. The largest of the diamonds in the hat (known as the Sancy diamond) is a fine jewel and its worth at the time can be inferred from the verdict of Philip de Commines, that it was the 'largest in Christendom'.

Flanders has the distinction of having produced some of the most magnificent of the embroideries created in Europe in the Middle Ages. Famous in all countries were the vestments of the Order of the Golden Fleece, an order which follows closely after the English Order of the Garter and was founded by Philip the Good on January 10th, 1430 on the occasion of his marriage to Princess Isabella of Portugal. The sovereign served as grand master of the Order and was attended by knights and gentlemen. When Charles v abdicated in 1556, the Order was controlled by the House of Austria and later in the eighteenth century when a dispute arose concerning the Order, the Emperor Charles vi took the archives to Vienna, where he also had transferred, as already noted, the sumptous embroideries of the Order.

The habit of members of the Order called forth the skill of the finest embroiderers. The surcoat was in rich red velvet and was lined with white silk. The cap was of purple ornamented with gold thread. The mantle of purple velvet had a white border embroidered on it and *pailletes* were sewn on to it. Tabards of the Order dating from the time of pillage at the Battle of Grandson are at the Historical Museum at Berne.

The more famous vestments of the Order of the Golden Fleece are described in the inventory of the Order written at the time of the death of Charles the Bold. A fairly accurate date of the completion of the embroideries can in this manner be ascertained.

The vestments formed a set of sacerdotal robes intended for use at High Mass. There are three big copes or pluvials, one chasuble, two vestments for servers, a dalmatic and a tunic and two antependia. The altar furnishings have had a chequered history. They were taken to Brussels where they remained for centuries. At the approach of the armies of the French Revolution, 1789, they were removed to Vienna for safety and were reunited once more to the other embroideries of the set.

The antependia have a foundation of coarse linen. On this gold thread is worked in couching stitch, the metallic threads being laid horizontally; flesh is worked in very fine split stitch. Blue, green and red silks in varying shades are used to represent draperies; and pearls are used lavishly.

The arrangement of the design is after the manner of altar triptychs for there is the traditional arrangement of a large central panel bordered by two smaller side panels. Scenes depicted show the Holy Trinity and the Mystical Marriage of St Catherine. The flesh representations set off against gold work are worked in split stitch 'in such a manner with such tender shading of tones, such melting into each other of threads that we can only imagine that we have before us an oil painting; almost more wonderful is the method of treating the gold threads'.

The priests' vestments are in crimson velvet and bear patterns arranged in hexagonals, the outlines of which are punctuated with rosettes set with pearls. As in the antependia, pearls are used in profusion on the hems of the vestments, on the borders and on the figures. Unfortunately, the sapphires and other precious stones adorning figures have been mutilated and lost during the vicissitudes to which the embroideries have been subject. On the neck of the cope, designs show the figure of Christ accompanied by Mary and John and in the background are choirs of angels and groups of saints. The chasuble carries scenes from the New Testament, the most prominent showing the baptism of Christ and his transfiguration. On the vestments of the servers, figures of saints both male and female are embroidered. All these pictorial designs were in the current pictorial tradition. The influence of the Flemish school of painting is apparent in the designs on the antependia. The designs on the vestments are attributed to Hubert and Jan Van Eyck though there is a school of thought which maintains that their originator was Roger van der Weyden. It is sufficient at the present time to recognize that the designs were inspired by Flemish artists at their best.

The *nué* technique employed in the creation of these embroideries has never been surpassed. Indeed the work was so excellent that it came to be known from then on as the Burgundian technique and was of such fine quality that silk experts have on occasions been at a loss in recognizing specimens as embroideries rather than as woven silk. Most specimens are worked in red in various shades, although many shades of blue were introduced, these being set off by the introduction of green, mauve and brown. The embroiderers achieved astonishing results with the introduction of shot silk, the glimmering shades of which made the rich embroideries resemble yet more closely contemporary Flemish paintings. The texture of the materials used and the reflections from the precious stones inserted into the work, contributed yet further to this effect.

During the Renaissance period, Flemish embroideries continued to flourish. The embroiderers now recognized the limitation of their materials and instead of emulating the Flemish painters they developed an individual technique and expressed themselves with greater restraint.

Many of the embroideries were made for the use of the church and the designs were inspired by those that appeared on the triptychs of the time; biblical scenes and symbols were pre-eminent. An ubiquitous motif was that of the Tree of Jesse with King David depicted in the centre.

Van Ysendeck in his *Classified Documents concerning Flemish Art in the 15th and 16th Centuries* treats the embroideries of this period. A particularly fine example of the embroidery of the Flemish Renaissance period was taken from the Abbey Grimbergen to the Royal Museum, Brussels. The arms of Christopher Outres, prior of the abbey during the period 1615–1647, are worked on the cloth and also the inscription *Panis confortans Christus*. The designs are separated from each other by columns or other architectural features and each scene represents Christ partaking of a meal. These are linked with biblical scenes such as that of the marriage feast at Cana, the meal at Bethany, that at the house of Simon the leper, the repast with Zacchaeus and that at Emmaus. Most prominent is the scene showing the Last Supper. The artistic effect of the scene is admirable. The proportions of the human figures are good and laws of perspective are observed. Moreover, the figures are alive and suggest action. Faces are worked in silk and the features are introduced successfully. There is sound dramatization in the representation of Christ who is sometimes shown at the centre of a group, sometimes at the side but always in possession of strategic influence and power. The architectural devices introduced to separate the scenes are designed in slight relief and the gold thread which enhances the columns and details of clothing enhances the total effect of work already excellent in itself.

II Eastern Europe

Much of the embroidery made in the countries of eastern Europe was domestic in character. Specimens that have survived from the Middle Ages are not sufficient in number, nor are they in so satisfactory a state of preservation, to allow for a reconstruction of the line of development in these countries. The older names of the countries are maintained in these references for they are the more familiar and are the appropriate labels by which many specimens in present day museums are catalogued.

The embroideries of England, Flanders and Italy are characterized by magnificence and were created with the blessings of the church, of kings and of a flourishing aristocracy. In complete contrast to this, the embroideries indigenous to eastern and central Europe were the outcome of popular expression. The embroideries represented art for the people by the people. Unhampered by dogma and symbolism, they evinced a freshness of style which appealed to all countries in all ages.

The range of work was so wide that to the present time it has defied complete analysis and classification. Certain features such as the quality of the materials used, peculiarities of technique and artistic clichés representing racial traits, unite groups of these embroideries. The similarity of specimens emanating from different countries has been accredited to a common origin resulting from communal tuition in specific convents. Moreover, the land-cultivating countries of Europe were averse to innovations and a design and technique once accepted was in all likelihood established.

As elsewhere in Europe, embroidery was classified into two main divisions. One type was based on the *material* on which it was worked (plate 66). Much European embroidery was worked on counted threads which was a comparatively easy method when working on hand-woven canvas or linen. Another type was freely worked embroidery (plate 65). Central and eastern Europe showed a distinct preference for the first type of work.

It is inevitable that in so great an area as that indicated, embroidery should show great diversity in characteristics, technique and colour harmonies. Moreover, at times, it is difficult to attribute an exact locality to certain types of work as there was constant migration of peoples along waterways such as the Danube and along land routes. When considering embroidery as a form of peasant art, it must be borne in mind that certain expressions of this were on a higher level than others. Whenever there was a powerful civilized centre, then peasant expressions tended to decay the more rapidly. Under the influence of Vienna, the peasant art of lower Austria sank into decay. Upper Austria on the other hand kept its regional traditions for a far longer period. Mountain ranges encircled certain areas and in these also old traditions of craftsmanship were retained.

Historical and geographical influences bound eastern Europe to the eastern end of the Mediterranean and to the countries bordering its shores. Peoples were linked by racial development, progress and retrogressions. Intercourse was strengthened by trade bonds, by travel and by religious and political persecutions. Craftsmen from Egypt, from Turkey, from Asia Minor, Greece, Albania, and from India and China and Persia were all united in a grand freemasonry.

To understand fully the value of embroidery in the eastern and central regions of Europe, one must acknowledge the importance given to embroidered linen in the home. Embroidered linens formed part of a woman's dowry. Much of it was used in her lifetime and a considerable portion was reserved to be handed on to the next generation as an heirloom. The sanctity afforded to such beautiful specimens has resulted in their preservation and the contents of many of the marriage coffers of earlier generations form collections in museums today.

A bride's trousseau included embroidered furnishings for her home and among the items bed curtains, pillow covers, bed spreads, window or shutter cloths and covers for consecrated baskets. Each of these had special meanings for the people using them and as a result the embroideries were characterized by distinct national trends. Racial history is evident in some of the motifs and the symbolism depicted denotes religious development. Motifs on the embroidered linens included fabulous animals and flowers while the accepted symbols of western Christianity found acceptance in regions where the Greek Church prevailed. Many of the household furnishings bore embroideries showing the Crucifixion, the Lamb and Flag and the Unicorn Chase. Bed curtains used at times of confinement are particularly interesting as indicative of local folk lore. Some of the motifs were embroidered in order to ward off the Evil One and to entice good spirits to the assistance of the newly-born child. Some of the pictorial scenes depicted are of value to the social historian for they indicate contemporary life, they show men and women bringing presents to the young child and depict also the service known as the Churching of Women.

Such household furnishings were usually worked in linen for they were in constant use and required frequent washing. Some were in silk and were worked in gold thread. Generally speaking, however, the furnishings were in linen although much of the stitchery was in wool. Colours varied according to districts and countries but there was a prevailing delight in reds, blues, light greens and black.

Beautiful as were the household linens, the national dress of the peoples was yet more beautiful (plates 67, 69). The use of these is waning but a colour-loving people still delight in their display on occasions of national festivity. National characteristics appeared inevitably in personal dress but certain features were common to all countries.

Women's head-shawls and caps were always items of prime importance. They were embroidered in various ways. Some bore stitchery in yarn or silk; others displayed drawn thread work and all were invariably edged with peasant laces. Folk customs attached themselves closely to items of national dress. A woman prided herself on making a cap *par excellence* for her daughter, who wore it at her wedding and then stored it away until the time she was buried. It was essential that she should have the cap on her head in her coffin, for by it the mother would be able to identify her daughter in the Hereafter. Over the cap a woman wore a head scarf which was often exquisitely embroidered in colours that toned with the embroideries of the main garment. Designs show individual expression and the stitches worked in silks and yarns dyed with natural dyes, retain their original wealth of colour. Large numbers of these shawls have escaped destruction as they were placed on altars as votive offerings by women praying to be blessed with children. The churches later made use of the scarves as antependia.

More elaborate than the scarves were the blouses worn as part of the national dress. Older blouses carry only a strip of embroidery on the sleeve but later ones have rich designs, strongly reminiscent of the East, covering sleeves and front of the garments. Blouses of the Slovak, Dalmatian and Moravian regions show elaborate drawn thread work. The voluminous folds of these blouses were held in place by broad belts. The belts of the Tyrolean areas stand out for their magnificence and originality.

The Dalmatians gave special honour to the bridal blouse and scarcely a square inch of the garment was left without a heavy covering of embroidery. By strange custom, the garment was covered over by a heavy jacket so that the elaborate work of the devoted embroiderer – the bride – was wholly concealed. In the Egerland district, the embroiderers were more economical of their output and reserved it for exposed areas of the sleeves. Most of the stitchery was in blue, worked either in silk or in cotton; designs were interlaced with yellow.

Blue silk or wool was used also in Carinthia although more modern trends show a preference for polychrome silks. There was a preponderance of work in gold and silver thread.

Oriental trends in design and colourings characterized much of the work done in Moravia (province of Austria) and also in Bosnia and Herzegovina (virtually a province of the Ottoman Empire). Designs were on the whole traditional and innovations were generally the result of the draughtsmanship of the village carpenter.

Alpine regions show a close affinity with German work both in design, technique and in the materials used. The tendency towards the creation of white embroideries indicates an outlook similar to that of the Slavic races. German influences are also evident in the many beautiful specimens created in Czechoslovakia (plate 69). In many regions the embroidery was dependent, not on the variety of stitches used, but on the varied interpretation of one stitch. The Czechoslovaks, however, showed a mastery over a wide diversity of stitches.

The designs and technique of Slovak embroideries make a special appeal to the student. Much of the embroidery resembles needlepoint lace and extensive use was made of drawn thread work. The stitchery was usually made in white silk and sections of the work were dyed yellow by means of a direct application of saffron and white of egg on to the completed work.

Moravian work shows a predilection for black and white. The gala blouse, for example, had a collar worked in black and white and fashioned after the manner of a sailor's collar. When the embroiderers resorted to other colours, they showed a marked fondness for red and yellow and metallic threads.

The Ruthenes also delighted in white embroideries and in work in coloured silks and yarns, working mainly in cross stitch with some fillings in satin stitch. They were also greatly attracted towards the use of coloured beads.

Hungarian embroiderers were skilled in embroidering not only linens but leather. The designs used on leather articles were later used on textiles. The national dress of Hungary is remarkably gay, it is elaborately embroidered, the main colours being red and black. The designs and technique of workmanship vary depending on whether the wearer is married or unmarried. Women's caps were elaborately decorated and their skirts were full and long, providing ample scope for ornamentation by the needle. Generally the skirt was gathered up in front to reveal an elaborately embroidered petticoat and an apron worn over the skirt also afforded scope for the embroiderer. Colours worked into the border indicate gradations of age, for older women have aprons embroidered in black and in green, middle-aged women favour yellow, while the young wear bright red borders. The blouses of the men were often embroidered in white.

Vitality characterizes the peasant art of central and eastern Europe. It is only during this century that full evaluation has been given to the more national and primitive craftsmanship of Europe. Once this recognition has been made however, it has become evident that herein lies a rich field of knowledge of the civilizing forces of the past and an inexhaustible field of inspiration for the future.

Rumanian embroidery

Rich and varied embroidery, deriving its inspiration from Nordic sources, is characteristic of Rumanian work. The peoples of the zone extending from Moldavia to Sweden and Norway and including the Ruthenes and Finns, have for centuries shown themselves dexterous in the execution of design and fertile in imagination in the creation of motifs. Much of their work was true peasant art and many of the patterns were geometric, based on the right angles formed by warp and weft. Designs tended to be abstract and formed a distinct contrast to the figural and naturalistic work of Italy and other countries bordering on the Mediterranean.

Considering the position of Rumania geographically, one realizes that its people were so placed that a virile and individual art was inevitable. The district was a meeting place for strongly contrasting forces: on the one hand, there were the influences of the vigorous Nordic races; on the other, there were the links, centuries-old, between the peoples of Rumania and the cultured nations of the Mediterranean sea board. The influence of the Orthodox Greek Church permeated expressions of peasant art particularly in the principalities of Moldavia and Wallachia. Ubiquitous Byzantine symbols and Greek crosses as motifs in embroidery reflect the teachings of the Orthodox Church. They are explained too by the influence of the Moslem doctrine which forbade the delineation of the human figure in art.

It is difficult to speculate as to the date when geometric patterns were first used in these regions for prehistoric remains in Bessarabia (in the extreme south-west of European Russia) and the valleys of the Danube show their use before man became civilized. Greek culture penetrated into the Balkans in the fifth century, while during the mediaeval period cloths woven in these lands were impressed directly by Byzantine patterns such as were known universally through their use in frescoes and mosaics.

With the close of the Middle Ages, crafts in Rumania took on a more individual character. During the Renaissance and post-Renaissance era the Orthodox Church and the nobles became direct patrons of Rumanian art in all its forms. Designs show, in a remarkable degree, the ebb and flow of historical influences. Conspicuous are the recurrence of Slav and Turkish influences which in turn shaped and re-shaped Rumanian forms of expression. Ever vigorous and serving as a common denominator among many historical vicissitudes were strong national characteristics which fortunately defied the onslaughts of foreign influences.

Embroidery made a special appeal to Rumanians for it was a means of expressing their intense love of colour. Clothing and household furnishings were adorned lavishly with coloured stitchery.

A study of the motifs created is a fascinating pursuit in that it reveals the racial characteristic of the Rumanian peoples. In one sense, such embroidery may be regarded as a social document, for historical events were recorded and details of the daily life of the Rumanians were depicted. Those people who fell under Slavonic rule were inclined more than all others to record in textile form definite events of national significance. Bright colours and ambitious motifs expressed joy in deliverance from some national crisis and such motifs of good fortune tended to become consolidated in the national catalogue, being in time transferred to some specific garment such as the dress of a bride. In spite of the freedom in the creation of designs peasant work tended to be decidely conservative. Patterns were simple in line and composition, which made them easy to copy, while possessing a certain elasticity which resulted in a healthy and virile development.

The names of the motifs are intriguing although they have but little significance today as the motifs to which they originally applied have changed, most of them tending towards stylization. A large number of the names can, however, still be understood for they refer to flowers and animals and to articles employed by the peasant in his daily work. Flower names show a distinct oriental influence. Conspicuous among others are the motifs much favoured in Turkish work, namely the rose, poppy and carnation. Fruits such as the plum and pineapple were also used. Animals and birds, too, gave rise to many names; among them were: frog's foot, little eye, crab's claw, horse's ear, ram's horn and sick chicken. Other motifs depicted were objects of peasant use and were termed horse-shoe, ladder, rake, shuttle, comb – each term having a special significance in embroidery. The origin of certain more poetic terms has become obscure to the research student of today although their connotation may have been clear to embroiderers who worked them a century or more after the time when the motifs were first created. These names have a humorous twist in themselves and among them are monk's legs, devil's knee, prince's bloom, little grape, labyrinth and woman in a temper. Significant too is the term *riuri* – rivers – which the Rumanians give to embroidery. In his *L'Art Du Paysan Roumain* Opresco has written, 'It is clear that the people used this term to compare the sinuous but often parallel patterns, which ran the full length of a piece of embroidery, with the streams winding through the valleys.'

Embroidery was allied to woven patterns. The accoutrements of the peasant's house were embroidered with geometrical motifs. Flowers were stylized and were surrounded with rosettes, circles, bird forms, animals and small figures. Curtains, cloths and towels bore not only motifs such as these but stripes which had been *woven* into the fabric. Towels were ornamented for ceremonial purposes. When a priest entered a house he was offered the traditional bread and salt upon an embroidered towel.

The rich and varied national dress served as an excellent vehicle for the display of embroidery. There has been much speculation recently as to the exact origin of the rich costumes worn by the Balkan peasants today at their fêtes and ceremonial gatherings. But general opinion seems to indicate that they are the copies of dresses which were worn by the noble classes of late mediaeval times and then bequeathed to their vassals. Be that as it may, the peasant embroiderers show their colourful stitchery to advantage. Moreover, not only were colour and design harmonious but the total effect was enhanced in that the work displayed was suited to the purpose for which it was intended.

Embroidery for dress purposes was worked on leather as well as on textiles. Geometrical patterns prevailed above all others and often served as a background for representations of fruits and flowers. Polychrome work was popular in most districts, particularly in Transylvania and Bukovina. The Balkan peasant was attracted greatly by colour. Hungarian influences penetrated among the peasants, resulting in work that emphasized colour harmonies. It is of interest to observe, however, that certain districts reacted adversely against colour medleys; Moldavian workers for instance delighted in monochrome embroidery and restricted themselves to green and blue.

It was traditional for the national costume to be worked at home by the women of the household although professional tailors and embroiderers were also employed in the villages. The fabric on which the embroidery was worked was hand-woven and was of a particularly fine texture in the white blouse worn by the women and shirt worn by the men. These garments followed a traditional format; they were cut on generous lines, their ample folds being controlled at the neck and wrists by rows of smocking. Borders were worked in cross stitch, striped effects were achieved by lines of stem stitchery while shadings were obtained by satin stitches. Solid squares were made with Holbein stitch. Zig-zag stitches were used lavishly for ground work while outlines were emphasized with stem stitches. Real ingenuity was shown in the combination of varied stitches and the Rumanian embroiderer showed herself an adept at wise selection. Restraint in the range of stitchery often produced happy results as is evidenced by some of the older specimens of Oltenian embroidery.

The colours most favoured were red, yellow, blue, green, orange and purple. Red was prime favourite and was used in all its shades from dark plum, called by the peasant 'rotten cherry shade' to the most vivid scarlet. These colours were set off by the hand-woven fabrics, made from the sheep's wool, from goat's hair, from silk, flax and cotton. It was only in the late nineteenth century that the custom arose of introducing relief into the darker embroideries by the introduction of metallic threads, beads and *paillettes*.

One must be discreet in discussing Rumanian embroideries and avoid generalization for their composition and lay-out is often regional. National dress itself was often controlled by locale. Nevertheless certain factors are fundamental and common to all, such as the *riuri* or borders which appeared along lines of the seams, shoulder pieces and collars. The spaces of a garment left vacant of embroidery then received advancing phalanxes of stitchery which came to an abrupt halt in accordance with a premeditated scheme. These phalanxes were not closely knit and carried rows of stylized flowers, crosses, rectangles and circles, all of which were enclosed with stripes. Where a space appeared too pronounced, interlacing stems and tendrils bearing leaves and rosettes would reach out, linking the unembroidered region to the whole. They served to break the sharp contrast between the ornamented and plain surfaces. Motifs with units of their design showing an upward trend, were used in vertical arrangements, while horizontal and flat geometrical patterns were used on saddles of the shoulders.

Regional traditions regarding arrangements and composition remained secrets long after disputes between localities had been forgotten.

In Bukovina the embroiderers prided themselves on their versatility, traditional geometric designs were linked together by trailing stems, sleeve embroidery revealed a certain regional arrangement whereby the motifs were grouped in three sections in order that all of the full sleeve should be united in the embroidery scheme. Red and blue were the predominant colours. The outlines of motifs were emphasized by the use of coloured yarns or beads. Black was used but little until the late eighteenth century for until then it was not a fast dye. But more recent work has revealed a distinct reaction in favour of its use.

Black and white was the favourite colour combination of the Oltenian embroiderers. In the more easterly districts, influenced by oriental tendencies, workers delighted in magnificent effects and to this purpose they introduced gold and silver threads and *paillettes* into their embroideries. This was seen at its best when worked on dark fabrics such as those used for voluminous skirts and trousers.

Transylvanian embroiderers shared with those of the Olt valleys a preference for subdued embroideries; blues and green were intermingled effectively. Moreover, there was a delight in combining weaving with ornamental stitchery.

All the work was done without set patterns, designs and colour combinations being memorized from one generation to the other, and at times work of one valley was copied wholesale by another. This copying was not slavish however and the virility and individuality of the embroiderer remain evident even in old specimens.

Viewing Rumanian embroidery collectively it becomes apparent that, in common with all other peasant embroideries, the work reveals the national characteristics of the people – their delight in colour and repetition – and the influences of other nations which have been in close contact with them. The richness of oriental culture and the virility of Slavonic forces all find their relative expression in Rumanian embroidery while each regional valley or area maintains its own decisive features. The motifs used are also a reflection of the influences of different periods such as the Middle Ages and the eastern expression let loose into Europe at the time of the Renaissance. The influence of the church and of feudalism are also here and permeating all is the spontaneity so characteristic of all Rumanian art.

12 Northern Europe

The early embroideries of northern Europe possess definite saga-like qualities. On to hand-woven textiles, women embroidered designs of historical personages, ships, castles, trees, flowers and geometrical motifs. Old traditions were carefully preserved as the centuries advanced. Radical differentiations manifested themselves more and more clearly and local idiosyncracies established themselves into a regional mode.

Russia preserved jealously an old tradition of skilled embroidery made with gold and silver threads. Her embroidery workshops at Kieff were internationally renowned and provided the more magnificent of the vestments used in the Greek and Latin churches. On the other hand, Russian peasant work shows a wide diversity of styles inevitable on account of the vast area of the land. In the north, embroiderers showed a close affinity with the Finns and white linen embroidery was favoured. Cross stitch and darned patterns characterized much of the embroidery of central Russia whereas in the south-eastern area influences prevailed resulting in oriental designs worked in brightly coloured silks and gold and silver threads. Coarse linen, the threads of which could be easily counted, was used in the more northerly regions and in the south, linen of very fine texture, silk or muslin were used.

In Norway there exists a deep reverence for all forms of craftsmanship; embroidery, knitting and lace making have all received careful attention. In the past there was a prevalence of white work and designs were inspired by old folk art such as was seen in the wood carvings of the church. National costume was elaborately embroidered in cross and flat stitches and colour harmonies were introduced. The motifs suggested the locale of the work; they included deer, symbols of the midnight sun, figures in native dress, bridal crowns and wreaths of native flowers. Specimens handed down through the centuries include wall hangings, pillow cases with flaps at either end. Other household furnishings include bed hangings. These were usually worked in satin stitch, the peasant woman preferring to count the threads rather than work over a stamped pattern. Basket covers with embroidered 'leaves' were much in vogue and carriage and sleigh cushions were also elaborately embroidered.

Norwegian work is characterized by fine colourings and renowned for its delicate shades of blue, its russet browns and yellows. These were – and still are obtainable – from native dyes distilled from the bark of trees, from plants and lichens. Norway did not excel in originality of designs but the embroidered work created there was attractive in execution. Embroidery was essentially a peasant craft there and where ideas were borrowed from more sumptuous work, they were subservient to the main trends of native interpretation.

White work was an important feature of the embroidery of Denmark. Danish workers excelled in a type of embroidery peculiar to their country viz. *Hedebo* work. The word is derived from *heden* or heath where the peasant workers plied their craft. The fabric on which they worked was hand-woven linen, a fact which partly explains the durable qualities of the work; stitchery was usually in natural or white, some drawn work was introduced and lace fillings formed another attractive feature. Motifs included geometrical forms, trees, flowers and animals worked in a conventionalized manner. Stitches were in the main flat stitches, worked in such a way that the texture of the fabric was varied in character when the work was complete. The lack of colour in the work was not noticeable for its attraction lay in the variety of stitches used.

Icelandic interest in textiles dated from early times. Embroidery designs include motifs representing the midnight sun, great bonfires, northern lights, coralled and roaming deer, lakes, mountains and rivers. As in the other northern countries the people delighted in the making of *rya* which was a coarse rug made with short pile and close knots. Originally meant as a bed cover, the rya was later promoted to the function of being a day spread or a rug and therefore lost its real significance. Designs on this pile work were inspired by embroidered samplers, cross stitch motifs being specially favoured.

Old specimens of Icelandic work may be seen in the museum at Reykjavik and the National Museum of Copenhagen and at Stockholm. Many of these are worked on groundworks of wool and of linen and sometimes of silk. The work is colourful and is often embellished with threads of gold and of silver. The Icelandic origin of the embroideries is evident from the nature of the motifs showing ships, weapons, native flora and fauna and pictorial designs based on mythology and history.

National dress received special attention from the embroiderer. It was usual for a bride to dress in black with a blouse ornamented on sleeves and shoulders with gold and silver embroideries. Trailing leaf designs were much in evidence and floral wreaths and garlands also graced the skirt of the ceremonial dress.

Swedish embroideries

Today the craftwork of Sweden enjoys a wide international reputation. Swedish textiles, displaying a high degree of artistic skill, have been produced for many centuries and to make a study of them would be to make a study of Sweden, geographically and historically. Woven into the warp and woof of the fabrics and forming an essential feature of the designs appearing on these are reflections of the influences guiding and developing a peasant race of high culture which is prosperous, fastidiously clean and motivated by powerful equalitarian principles.

The embroidered fabrics of Sweden are not confined merely to those required for royal, civic and ecclesiastical functions, though the number of these is high and there are innumerable specimens of very real worth bequeathed from the past. Rather more interesting are those products, colourful, attractive and vigorous, which have been prepared by a peasant people for peasant life. These products include in the main native garments, especially those for ceremonial occasions, and furnishings for the peasant home. On these fabrics Scandinavian traditional patterns were embroidered and displayed in all their vitality. Examining these designs one is struck immediately by the Swede's great love for his own country and throughout the centuries designers have clung tenaciously to definite forms in folk art. As lovers of their own countryside, the designers looked for motifs around them and depicted on the fabrics designs of plants, birds, animals and flowers. The more advanced designers of today have not forsaken the old tradition and they seek inspiration in the carved work displayed so generously in the country churches of Sweden, in the paintings of the peasantry and in the chip carvings preserved in so very many

Swedish farmsteads.

These patterns are not so uniform or so stereotyped as one might be inclined to think, reflecting that Sweden has in the main a homogenous population which has been comparatively secure from foreign incursions and invasions. Geography and climate have played a powerful part in the development of craftwork in all its forms. An individual style is evident in each of the Swedish provinces extending from Vasterbotten by way of Dalarnia Väster-Gotland, Uppland to the Southern Provinces of Skåne, Blekinge and Småland and the Baltic Islands of Oland and Gotland. European influences penetrated the more southerly provinces and consequently what may be termed a more truly Swedish native style is that in evidence in the more northerly Värmland, Vastmanland and Dalarna.

The peasant culture was influenced by the more sterotyped culture of the so-called upper classes – the clergy, the nobility and burghers. This was subject to all the influences common to other European nations and it is interesting to observe that these influences were strong in Sweden at an early date, they were very active in the Middle Ages and grew in volume and staying power with the coming of the Renaissance. During the seventeenth and early eighteenth centuries British, Dutch, Italian and French influences in turn affected Swedish craftwork. This, the era of Carl X, Carl XI and Carl XII was known as the Carolingian period. Under Carl XI when the aristocracy became subservient to the rising middle class, the traits of art favoured by the commercially minded Dutch and British people replaced the more artistic and exotic French style.

During the great wars of Carl XII, craft work fell into abeyance but there was a virile resuscitation under Frederick I (1720–1750). Trade with China developed and Sweden, like other European countries, showed a strong penchant for oriental fabrics and designs. Here is a very striking instance of the imitative qualities of peasant work. Embroiderers of the southern provinces in particular showed a lively interest in the colourful fabrics of the East and copied them not slavishly but with vigour, shaping them into designs that harmonized with the traditional patterns which they usually employed.

Returning to the fabrics of the upper classes we find that after 1732 French rather than English rococo was predominant. This is accounted for partly by changing taste and also by the fact that direct influence emanated from Stockholm where French craftsmen were employed in the decoration of the palace. It signifies to the virility and resourcefulness of the Swedish workers that they evolved a new style which may be appropiately termed Swedish rococo. This, in turn, inspired Swedish peasant workers who were attracted in particular by the rich colourings, the more varied materials and the floral patterns.

Swedish rococo did not prevail for long and was superseded by a modified French style. The Swedes called their adaptation of the Louis XVI style the Gustavian style after King Gustav III. There was an early Gustavian style lasting from *circa* 1770 to 1780, then there was a transitional period between 1780 and 1790 when the late Gustavian style became established and remained dominant until about 1810. The early period was characterized by work in delicate colours which seemed all the more attractive in contrast to the rich and distinctive colours of the rococo period that had gone before. Yet more subdued and infused with the powerful appeal of simplicity of line and colouring was the work produced in the late Gustavian period, a style which was readily accepted in all the provinces and which remained powerful throughout the first quarter of the nineteenth century.

More elaborate, but far less penetrating, was the new style which followed it. The 'Karl

138

Johan' style flourished between 1810 and 1830 and was a modification of the French Napoleonic style. It was not wholly acceptable to Sweden but its prevalence is explained by the authority of the Crown Prince Charles Jean Bernadotte, who was established in the country by Napoleon.

Industrialization took its toll of Sweden though, compared with many other countries, the nation was able to avoid many of the evils of an industrial revolution. By good fortune, Sweden had abundant water power and a balanced economy and although the new order cut deeply into traditional ways of life, enough stamina was left in the Swedes to counteract those forces which threatened to engulf their individuality.

The *Svenska Hemslöjds foreningarnas Riksforbund* – The National League of Swedish Homecraft Association and the *Svenska Hemslöjd* – Swedish Homecraft Association have worked unremittingly and successfully for the preservation of native technique and designs. In addition, they have ensured for textile handworkers as well as other craftsmen a populace appreciative of the arts and enlivened with a strong sense of local tradition and a sense of privilege in the care of craftsmanship for the present and for the future.

Turning to the alluring subject of peasant fabrics one is tempted to turn aside into the many by-paths offered by this study. One must be content, however, to refer in a more general way to the characteristics of certain of the provinces. The maritime provinces of the south showed themselves sympathetic to European influence whereas the seafaring people of Blekinge, because of their commercial undertakings, became directly acquainted with the designs and technique of the East. The designs created at Blekinge were not exact imitations, they were adapted and interwoven with traditional motifs, geometric patterns and legendary symbols. But Blekinge in turn influenced Gotland.

When examining Swedish embroidery one has to safeguard against becoming absorbed in the very fascinating study of pattern-weavings at which the Swedes were highly skilled. The handloom was a prominent fixture in most Swedish homes and the traditional patterns were woven in contrasting threads into the fabric. Embroidery was often used as an additional embellishment in the form of a border or subsidiary decoration on some cloths. Often too it was used as the only adornment on homespun fabrics of very fine texture which testified to the skill and capability of the spinner and weaver.

Some woven fabrics with embroidery have been preserved from the Viking Age (800–1050) but the evidence is too scanty to deduce information concerning the methods and motifs in use at the time. Fabrics of the thirteenth century have varied designs which have become traditional in succeeding ages. Early designs show a tendency to embroider and also weave motifs that had a personal and therefore historical significance to the worker. Queen Matilda and her ladies-in-waiting, perhaps, working the Bayeux Tapestry, had their counterparts in Sweden where women recorded on cloth the heroic deeds of their menfolk. Old Swedish embroideries and woven cloths preserve old Swedish legends and they are documents of worth to the social historian with their many motifs showing figures in contemporary costume, castles and ships.

Many of the old embroideries were on a lavish scale for they were meant for display on parade occasions. As Christianity penetrated into all the provinces biblical designs were favoured. Prominent throughout the ages on Swedish fabrics have been representations of Adam and Eve and of the wise and foolish virgins. Legendary motifs were retained and given a symbolic meaning in the early age of Christianity; the tree, for instance, was a prominent feature in Scandinavian mythology as the symbol of life and it appeared as a central feature in Adam and Eve scenes as a representation of the tree of the knowledge of good and evil. In later ages, the tree diminished to the size of a shrub and at times it was represented by a border of leaves only.

Many of the early Swedish embroideries are reminiscent of early Flemish tapestries with a groundwork gay with flowers. The lily was a favourite motif. Tulips and roses and all the flowers of the Swedish countryside were worked in gay colourings. Native birds and animals were also shown, the most usual of the latter being the reindeer.

Geometric patterns were very common, often inspired by the perfection of the woven fabric so characteristic of early Swedish textiles. Crudeness of implements and of materials in no way hampered the home-weavers, who prided themselves on the sureness of their technique.

An insight into traditional Swedish life will reveal both the purposes and the stability of embroidered work from the Renaissance period onward. Fabrics were woven in wool and in linen at home and became possessions of sentimental as well as of intrinsic worth. They were embroidered with motifs traditional to the district and often bearing modifications representing personal judgement, recollection and taste. Garments and furnishings were made with the intention that they should serve for more than one generation, so that when it became necessary to replace them, the new garment or furnishing fabric was modelled as closely as possible on the one that had become worn. In this manner patterns were preserved for generations. Personal interpretation of the traditional motifs kept them from becoming fixed and dormant.

Old Swedish homes were fitted with small windows, thus the housewife was restricted in her use of window curtains. She found compensation in working elaborate borders, beautifully embroidered and fringed with cuttings from her looms, and these she placed above the window and on the edges of shelves. The raftered ceiling, however, gave her more scope to display her handwork, woollen and linen material was woven at home to the required dimensions of the space between two rafters and patterns were often woven into the linen. Many ceiling cloths were made according to the *krabbasnar* technique, embroidered motifs being added to the woven design. Cloths were usually made of natural linen and dark red wool. The motifs embroidered were of ancient usage, many of them bearing a close resemblance to the designs used for adornment in the Viking Age. Mythological figures were much in evidence and the unicorn and basilisk were among heraldic beasts. Biblical figures were encircled with floral wreaths, the whole being bound with borders, bearing motifs such as peacocks with fantastic tails, stars and the Christian monogram I.H.S.

The wall beds had no shutters but were fitted with an embroidered curtain or curtains that could be drawn. The designs on these matched the border on the white linen spread upon the bed and the coverlet on top of the spread was usually worked in gay colours. A separate piece of embroidery was worked and attached to the ends of the pillow cases. Above the bed head hung a white linen towel on which embroidery was worked above the fringed end. The embroidery work on the bed furnishings usually matched, the whole forming a bed set and another towel similar to that near the bed hung near the entrance as a symbol of hospitality. The only time it was ever used was along with four others for carrying a coffin out of the house. A large number of the motifs were worked in satin and in stem stitch, while others were worked in cross stitch, always by means of the counted thread for patterns were disdained.

Tablecloths were also embroidered, the more elaborate ones being used for state occasions. A special cloth was reserved for the clergyman's annual visit; a square was worked in this to indicate where the clergyman would sit to catechize the household.

Embroidered cushions lent colour and gaiety to the Swedish home. On a groundwork of natural linen or on black, dark blue or green cloth or else on red homespun, designs would be worked in coloured wools. Floral patterns were popular for cushions and they were arranged much after the usual Renaissance fashion with big blooms in each corner and a wreath with initials and date in the centre. Animals and biblical figures were also introduced and would appear from among the boldly curving stems or exotic blooms.

Appliqué work was very popular on cushions; the small sections of material were embroidered with bright threads and would then be attached to a dark ground. Coloured threads would be used to secure the pieces to the cushion and the attaching stitches themselves, in the form of rows and rows of chain stitch, contributed considerably to the total effect. Other cushions were made in patchwork and much ingenuity was displayed in the assembling of pieces.

Each chair had its special cushion and this was used only on special occasions. Cushions such as bridal cushions, were made in pairs and were used for kneeling at the altar in the wedding ceremony. They bore the initials of bride and bridegroom and the father of each was indicated. K.R.D. indicated the name of Kristin Ronders Dotter or Daughter; P.N.S. that of Pers Niels Son. Other embroidered work might have the initial H before the initials of the name indicating that the worker was a *Husfru* or married woman; the initial J stood for *Jungfru*, a spinster.

Cushions were made for carriages, sleighs and saddles. Pewter threads added an original touch to many of these. At times the embroiderer would confine herself to the use of wools in natural colours, white, black and grey, but Swedish love of colour is strong and bright dyed threads were judiciously introduced.

The garments used by the peasantry were made from fabrics spun and fashioned at home and the housewife embroidered them herself. Each person prided himself or herself on the possession of fine church-going clothes and state clothes. Garments were voluminous and numerous. Status and wealth were revealed by the number of skirts and of trousers donned for wearing at the same time. The head-dresses worn by married women displayed beautiful embroidery and smocks of both men and women were elaborate. It was the custom for the bride to present her groom with a shirt which she wove in the finest linen and was meticulous in embroidering the collar, cuffs and shirt front. The groom accepted it as a labour of love, ignored the fact that it was an ill fit and accepted the garment although it had been begun long before the girl had known him. In return, he would present her with embroidered mittens which he had commissioned at the market place to be made for her hands and for no other. These were of knitted fabric with conventional patterns woven in and embroidered in coloured wools and pewter thread.

13 *America*

Embroidery in America derived its main traditions from the early settlers. Pioneer women showed a determined effort to uphold graceful and dignified elements in life and to foster a virile, artistic expression as the new nation was being forged.

In the early years of settlement women were restricted by their lack of materials. But they met the challenge and produced the supplies by hand. The rhythmic purring of the great wool-wheel with its continuous droning was a familiar sound in an early colonial kitchen. Around its walls, ready to hand, hung yarn reels, wheel fingers, card reeds, distaffs and knots of coloured yarn. The sheep wool was washed, spun, skeined, dyed and cut into convenient strands for use in crewel work. Much ingenuity was shown in obtaining vegetable dyes. Wool, for instance, was dyed in a wide variety of colours, – blue being the most prevalent, made from home-grown indigo and tinted to various degrees by immersion. The early settlers also wove linen yarn which was much used in embroidery and older specimens show embroidery worked on narrow strips of linen, necessitated by small looms. As spinning machinery advanced, hand-spun linen was replaced by mechanically spun cotton which was much cheaper and more easily available.

The first settlers were concerned with the utiliarian needs of needlework. Further, in a primitive environment there was very little need to practise the art of embroidery. Where decorative stitchery was introduced, threads were very colourful, sometimes bizarre; though time has tempered much garishness in specimens which have survived the centuries. Designs and stitches for several generations showed a tendency to conservatism; what had been practised in the Old World was transferred to the New. There was a distinct clinging to the past and no special desire to incorporate any of the new expressions of art, tent stitch was still usual on furnishings and decorative designs, mainly of a geometrical nature, were worked in cross stitch.

Even more common than the embroidered picture in the American home of today is another treasure of the past – the sampler. Pictures and samplers resemble each other so closely that it is often difficult to differentiate between them; but pride of ancestry usually steps forward to point out and emphasize the signature and date which are almost inevitably inscribed on a sampler. Children in the early Puritan homes worked assiduously at their samplers. Some of the most celebrated of these children's samplers are those of Anne Gower, first wife of Governor Endicott, in the Essex Institute, Salem, and that of the daughter of the Puritan leader, Miles Standish – the Sampler of Loara Standish which is dated 'born 1623' (Pilgrim Society of Plymouth, Massachusetts).

Today the sampler is valued as a piece of needlework in itself and its original purpose has become obscured by time. The sampler worked by children's diligent fingers, with its rows of alphabets, numerals, tree of life, stereotyped figures and inscribed with biblical and didactic verses was originally a substitute for the rare pattern book. This explains why samplers are worked in a variety of stitches. Early samplers are narrow, for the looms on which the linen was woven were narrow and, because of this, they seldom have the borders which are such elaborate features of later samplers.

With time the sampler became a primer for the young; for instance there developed the map sampler for instructing children in geography. For adult workers, the sampler broadened out to portray landscapes and figures dressed in contemporary clothing which were enclosed in geometric or floral borders. By the eighteenth century, the sampler had become particularly elaborate, verses, alphabets and pictorial scenes vied with each other for a place on the canvas and a local touch was often introduced into the borders which carried designs of native flowers.

Late seventeenth century and early eighteenth century pictures are of importance as social documents for many women have recorded with their needles valuable information concerning contemporary life and the folklore of a neighbourhood: designs of flowers and fruits were inspired by the gardens of the embroiderers, fantastic designs of seaweeds and mermaids were worked within borders of shells, national history was embroidered and symbols such as stars and shields and eagles testified to political creeds and religious beliefs. Much of the work was done on burlap and though the colours are often still crude, the total work invariably possesses a native charm (plates 80, 81).

Establishments providing education for young ladies prided themselves on the gentility and the versatility of the curriculum they offered. Embroidery lessons were emphasized. A Boston schoolmaster, Mr Bromwell, advertising in 1716 stated:

> Young Gentlewomen and children are taught all sorts of fine works, as Feather Works, Filigree and painting on Glass, *Embroidery*, A New Way, Turkey Work; for Handkerchiefs, two New Ways; fine new Fashion purses, flourishing and plain work.

Every accomplished young lady was expected to be skilled in embroidery for therein was her insignium of a sound education. A book entitled *Pencil Sketches* written by Eliza Leslie and published in 1835 tells how one of the characters, Mrs Almore, brought her daughter to a fashionable drawing school in Philadelphia. In testifying to the skill of her daughter she tells the principal:

> 'She has been four quarters with Miss Julia and has worked Friendship and Innocence with cost upwards of a hundred dollars.' Then the proud Mother queries, 'Do you know the piece, Mr Gammage? There is a tomb with a weeping willow and two ladies with long hair, one dressed in pink, the other in blue holding a wreath between them over the top of an urn. The ladies are Friendship. Then on the right hand of the piece is a cottage and an oak and a little girl dressed in yellow sitting on a green bank and putting a wreath around the neck of a lamb. Nothing can be more natural than lamb's wool. It is done entirely in French Knots. The child and the lamb are Innocence.'

In the celebrated school of Mrs Isabella Graham in New York, young ladies of the republic were taught embroidery by competent instructors. Embroidery became the pastime of the leisured mistresses of large households. Mrs Washington embroidered twelve chair cushions, four for each of her three grand-daughters; she worked on coarse canvas using designs of shells worked in brown and yellow wools and introducing highlights with gold coloured silks.

Inventories supply evidence that life was not so plain and austere as it has become customary to think of it in the Puritan states. Turkey work was fashionable there too. It was used for church furnishings, and for the wooden chairs and benches of the homes of the colonists. Scripture texts were embroidered on shirts. Tent stitch was taught in Boston and was used on work calling for considerable detail. One Boston shopkeeper advertized that he taught 'Dresden and Embroidery on gauze, Tent Stitch and all sorts of coloured work'.

Crewel work (see plate 78) of the Jacobean type, familiar in England, became established in America. The freshness and grace of the new designs depicting strange or amusing animals, birds of magnificent plumage and luxuriant flowers were eagerly welcomed for furnishings, bed hangings, curtains, cloths and cushions but with time these were adapted to suit the taste of the new land. In the main the oriental designs of birds and beasts and flowers remained unchanged but the American needleworker tended to dispense with the more orthodox stitches – satin, feather, herringbone, rope, coral, feather, cable and flame stitch. Instead she worked her designs in outline, producing a gayer, lighter effect. With time many designs were simplified – the tree of life was reduced to a triangle; motifs were detached and spaced at intervals on a plain background. Mary Breed of Breed's Hill, outstanding in Revolutionary History, worked on a bedspread showing designs, completely out of proportion, of flowers and animals (Pennsylvania Museum of Art). Marian Webb of Connecticut confined her efforts to a bed valance in 1756 and she too over-emphasized motifs showing Indian flowers. These flowers graced the wedding dress of Mary Meyers in the year 1732 (Connecticut Historical Society, Hartford). Buds from the Orinoco Valley inspired designs for a bedspread in Plymouth about the same time and there is documentary evidence concerning a valuable petticoat which was stolen from its Boston owner in November 1749; this had a 'large work'd Embroidered Border, being Deer, Sheep, Houses, Forests Etc., so worked'. At Bridgehampton the remains of a bed set worked in 1779 was discovered. There are indications that there were Indian floral motifs but the main design has unique interest and the embroidery is undoubtedly the work of revolutionary fingers, the figures worked being unmistakably caricatures of British soldiers.

Quilting as practised in England, France and Holland was done at an early period in America. Quilting parties or 'bees' were held usually before haymaking or after it was over. Candlewick embroidery, knotting and couching was used and designs were often local and became traditional. The names are often quaint and picturesque – Blue Bell, Sweet Briar, The Bird in a Tree, The Bowl of Snowballs. Designs were later taken from women's magazines.

As materials became more abundant the thrifty housewife turned to the making of appliquéd quilts which lent themselves to much embroidery stitching. Some of the quilts worked in this way have a definite historical value for they were worked in critical periods of the nation's development. During the Harrison-Tyler campaign the Whig Rose and Democrat Rose designs were worked and roses symbolized political feeling during the Civil War. Then there was the Harvest Rose and Prairie Rose expressing the spirit of westward expansion. During the nineteenth century the Rose of Sharon was the most popular design.

The Bible inspired a number of picturesque designs, among which the most popular were Noah's Dove, The Tree of Life, Solomon's Crown, Steps to the Altar and The Rose of Sharon. There were series of stars e.g. Star of Texas, and The Rising Sun, The Blazing Sun and The Hour Glass. There were local names such as The Rocky Glen of The Mountain States and The Lost Ship of the Coast; The Bear's Paw of Ohio and The

Hand of Friendship of the Quakers of Philadelphia.

Boston Museum of Fine Arts possesses embroidered quilts bearing autographs; names are embroidered on squares, sometimes these represent a financial effort. 'Get your name on for a dime.' One quilt has 2,780 pieces and 556 autographs.

Then there was the patchwork quilt made up of oddments of material sewn together, very often with decorative stitches. Personal and family history was frequently traced in an heirloom quilt as a portion of a bridal dress or baby's robe was stitched in. Here again patchwork has historical value. One of which there is record is the work of Miss Mary Langden of Portsmouth, New Hampshire and other fair ladies of that town. They held a quilting bee and made a flag for John Paul Jones which he flew defiantly as the *Bon Homme Richard* sank. The girls had made the flag from silken strips from their best gowns; the three white strips in the New Constellation were cut from the bridal dress of Mary Seavey. The resulting banner was, by tradition, the first edition of the Stars and Stripes to be saluted by the guns of an European naval power. The making of a silk crazy quilt made by sewing scraps of material haphazardly together was a very usual pastime in the nineteenth century. The completed seams were often covered over with feather stitching. Such was the vogue that American textile manufacturers sold kits of materials for the purpose; these included an assortment of silks, designs, sometimes templates and instructions.

Tambour work had its devotees especially at the time of the Civil War when women, using a frame, worked at what they called 'raised embroidery' on net. The work was done sometimes in the coarsest embroidery cotton or sometimes in wool when it appeared as raised dots. The technique resembled darning and designs were adapted for counterpanes, antimacassars and window curtains. The work had a definite status as needlework and a reference to it in *Peterson's Magazine* 1854 describes it as 'a style of work recently introduced from France known as Opus Anglicanum'.

A Mrs Sarah Hussey teaching in Philadelphia inserted an advertisement in the *Pennsylvania Packet* 1775 stating that she embroidered waistcoats in tambour work 'with or without gold'. When machine net became available in the nineteenth century, it was used extensively for tambour work. The technique was applied to a wedding veil dated 1825 and was also used on hand-run veils and scarves. Coloured silks applied to both black and white net were acclaimed as resembling Spanish bobbin-made laces. Indian muslins were embroidered in white for baby clothes, wedding attire and garments for older people. The designs were comparatively simple: vine leaves and oak patterns were worked on aprons. Collars were embroidered with borders of berries and leaves and muslin caps had small motifs in satin stitch and French knots. Motifs were sometimes worked in realistic detail and then they were applied to a foundation cloth.

Embroidery in America continued to flourish. Some of the finest influences came in the eighteenth century from the Moravian School established at Bethlehem, Pennsylvania in 1749. The schools of the Moravian Sisters spread into southern states and with them the practice of fine needlework. The range of work which was taught as an extra 'for seventeen shillings and sixpence, Pennsylvania currency' was wide. It included fine needlework and tambour work, ribbon work, crêpe work, flower embroidery and pictures on satin. The flower embroidery of the Moravian schools was particularly exquisite, using black twisted silk threads and lustrous flosses on satin of fine quality or eastern silks, soft yet strong. The specimens of the Moravian schools which survive provide ample evidence of meticulous work and artistic claims.

One such specimen is the banner of Count Casimir Pulaski who is commemorated in Longfellow's *Hymn of the Moravian Nuns* and this is now preserved by the Maryland Historical Society. Tradition has it that Pulaski during the American Revolutionary War recruited part of his famous Legion at Bethlehem. He ordered a banner to be made at the Moravian school. This was carried by his men until his death at the siege of Savannah in 1779. Some of the work of the early Moravian schools is preserved by the New York Society of Decorative Art. Flower embroidery prevails. Satin stitch was usual for small groupings, relief being sometimes introduced by 'stuffing' of cotton floss and larger flowers were created in tent stitch later to become known as 'Kensington'. Some of the cushions embroidered were also inscribed and one that has survived bears an inscription in copperplate writing 'Wrought where the peaceful Lehi flows', words raising nostalgic thoughts of a Bethlehem lying peacefully in a secluded valley while elsewhere the builders of a new nation were working strenuously.

The Moravian sisters also fostered the taste for picture embroidery which was to take so firm a hold on America and to become a part of the general American inheritance. The pictures were seldom more than twenty inches square, the size being regulated by the width of the beautiful satin which formed the background. Biblical scenes prevailed; many of these were inspired by prints; occasionally the embroidery was worked over such a print. The more skilled embroiderers worked on original designs, some of these being the work of skilled artists. The early Moravian work of the late eighteenth and early nineteenth centuries was the work of young ladies of gentility. The influence of the Moravian sisters was, however, wide. It has been maintained that 'Bethlehem was the source of the most skilful needlework art in America'. The work represents a romantic period of American embroidery which contrasted vividly with the crewel embroidery which preceded it and with the muslin embroidery of the New England states. Candace Wheeler in her book *The Development of Embroidery in America* writes:

> The influence of the Bethlehem teaching lasted long enough to build up a very fine and critical standard of embroidery in America. It would be difficult to overestimate the importance of the influence of this school of embroidery upon the needlework practice of a growing country. Its qualities of sincerity, earnestness and respect for the art of needlework gave importance to the work of hands other than that of necessary labour and these qualities influenced all the various forms of work which followed it.
>
> The first divergence from the original work was in its application, rather than its method, for instead of having a strictly decorative purpose its application became almost exclusively personal. Flower embroidery of surpassing excellence was its general feature and the materials for the development of this form of art were usually satin, or the flexible undressed India silk which lent itself perfectly to ornamentation. Breadths of cream-white satin, of a thickness and softness almost unknown in the present day, were stretched in Chippendale embroidery frames, and loops and garlands of flowers of every shape and hue were embroidered upon them. They were often done for skirts and sleeves of ceremonial gowns, giving these an even greater distinction than the flower brocades so much coveted by colonial belles.

Another type of embroidery which flourished in America at much the same time was what became known as 'French embroidery'. There was no organized school of such work but it seeped into the new and virile continent from many sources; although termed 'French' this type of work also flourished in England and the close connection between England and France at this time may have contributed in a measure to the strength of its influence. During the period approximately 1750 to 1840 French embroidery enjoyed a great vogue in the States and a very large number of specimens has survived from this period, giving ample evidence of the skill and the charm of the work.

A variety of muslins, cambrics and linens was used for the work, the more costly linen-cambrics and India mulls being reserved for superior work. Flosses of linen or cotton were used as threads. Stitches were simple, the most usual being an over and over stitch. Relief was sometimes introduced by underthreads. Designs were seldom original; they were usually copied from 'bought work' which was often imported from France or England.

Articles of personal wear were exquisitely embroidered and in days of flowing draperies, a gown would be embroidered from the neck to the hem of a long train. Collars, capes and pelerines were embroidered and many a young girl spent many months embroidering her own wedding dress. Baby clothes gave a wide opportunity for the practice of French embroidery and baby caps received special attention. Christening robes, sometimes with a six foot train, were beautifully embroidered in the sure knowledge that they would become family heirlooms. Moreover, at this period of time American men favoured finely stitched shirts and exquisite ruffles and so these too gave scope for the nimble fingers of the embroideress. With time, progress was made from the over and over stitch to an elaborate network of lace stitches and hem stitches. Open work or perforated work became usual, a bodkin, 'piercer' or darning needle being employed for the purpose.

French embroidery was replaced by a type of embroidery which had, for a considerable period of time, existed alongside it. This was Spanish lace work which was used lavishly on shawls and on large lace veils which were graceful accessories of colonial and early American costume. It flourished first in the southern states having come from Mexico by way of New Orleans. Foliated designs were worked on fine lace a yard square for veils; whereas shawls were usually larger and the lace correspondingly heavier in texture. Lace stitches were worked into the mesh of the ground fabric. Darning on net was also usual and designs usually took the form of wreaths or basket-flowers. Edges were scalloped and there were 'powderings' of flower-buds. Exquisite wedding veils were made; orange flowers were embroidered in silk flosses and rich flower wreaths ornamented borders. Silver flosses were embroidered effectively on black net.

The vogue for needlework pictures (plate 77) continued throughout the eighteenth and nineteenth centuries and they were worked in wool or wool and silk on canvas. Tent stitch, cross stitch and other canvas stitches were also used and there was now a wide range of designs: classical, biblical and scenic. Contemporary paintings served as inspiration for many and the finest work for these was made in silk floss which contained a little chenille and tiny pieces of silver thread were introduced to brighten effects. Some of these pictures are a compromise; they show work in embroidery stitches and in watercolours, the latter contributing to an economy of labour and of expense. Of contemporary painters of the early nineteenth century, Angelica Kauffmann was the most influential. Embroidered patterns sold made embroidery work much easier. The 1859 Godey's *Lady's Book* refers to stamp transfers made by Alfred Pierce of Masillon, Ohio.

A quotation from Oliver Wendell Homes reads:

> Take your needle, my child, and work at your pattern; it will come out a rose by
> and by. Life is like that – take one stitch at a time, taken patiently and the pattern
> will come right out like embroidery.

Nineteenth century embroidery in America, as in England, had as its most characteristic feature Berlin wool work, which was known in the USA as 'Zephyrs' and was
applied to every conceivable object, more especially furnishing but to costume also. Wools
in bright German taste were used, cross stitch and petit point were used and so was a
'clipped stitch' which created a soft raised pile which contributed well to shading.
Chenille and especially glass beads were added to the design and the finished article was
often weighed down with showy cords and tassels.

One adaptation of Berlin work was cardboard embroidery termed 'Bristol Boards'. The
stitchery was done on cardboard on which a design had been drawn or painted; mottoes
and texts were usual and greeting cards were also worked in this method and later framed.
Berlin work had its devotees – and also its detractors.

The Husband's Complaint

I hate the name of German wool
   In all its colours bright.
Of chairs and stools in fancy work
   I hate the very sight
The rugs and slippers that I've seen
   The ottomans and bags;
Sooner than wear a stitch on me
   I'd walk the street in rags.

Oh Heaven preserve me from a wife
   With 'fancy work' run wild
And hands which never do ought else
   For husband or for child;
Our clothes are rent our bills unpaid
   Our house is in disorder
And all because my lady wife
   Has taken to embroider.

Peasant embroideries of the Old World were transferred to the New. The Industrial
Revolution brought about the production of cheap mass-produced clothing and the
consolidation of main groups of the population in the towns. The traditional patterns
of national costume were abandoned but fortunately many specimens have survived to
become by today rich areas for research by the sociologist and also by the embroiderer.

Original materials were hand-woven and designs were based on the counted thread:
based on these facts, embroiderers in the USA copied work traditional to their own native
countries and adapted them to modern needs. Religion played its part in the continuance
of these national patterns and techniques. Embroideries were used in church ceremonials
and festivals among people of many religions, whether they were Orthodox Greek or
Orthodox Russian, Roman Catholic, Ukrainian, Syrian, Jewish or Moslem. The embroideries were individual and, by their purpose, tended to keep people apart. In the
modern trend towards church unity however, it is interesting to note work in church
embroidery in America today. By tradition of design, it links people who are 'still a
nation within a nation' with the country of their ancestry rather than divides them by
religious custom and new links are constantly being forged in this sphere across the
Atlantic.

Washington Cathedral, set high above the Potomac River and founded only fifty years
ago, is unique in that it is already working out a conception of uniting many Christian

traditions. There are outstanding links with many nations in sculpture, stained glass and carvings. Furthermore there are already five hundred embroideries. These include ecclesiastical vestments, fine linen and church furnishings. There are many kneelers and cushions and rugs. The choir stalls have the shields of the various dioceses of America. A rug for the High Altar was worked in 22 pieces and carries the rich colours of the Sanctuary windows. A bronze Jerusalem cross which is shown on the face of the Altar is repeated in the centre of the rug. The Bishop's Chair has a cushion with the Arms of Glastonbury. A Tudor Rose motif on it appears on the matching kneeler. The various chapels have been given kneelers worked with special designs and a current project raising much interest is one commemorating the lives of American presidents from George Washington onward.

Not only in Washington but in countless other churches an effort is being made to make national religious buildings beautiful with embroidery (plate 82 and 83). The Church of the Ascension, Middletown, Ohio and also the Church of the Redeemer at Brynmawr are but two among very many with ambitious artistic and technical schemes.

As mentioned earlier, with the coming of the machine age embroidery in America lost many of its national characteristics. Machine-made fabrics stilted initiative; products – textiles of all kinds – came to America from all parts of the world; women's emancipation from the home led to wider interests and there was a decrease in certain aspects of leisure.

The closing years of the nineteenth century witnessed a new spurt in handicrafts; William Morris of England and his mediaevalists had pioneered with his printing press and tapestry looms and his influence reached America. Groups of public-spirited people gathered and in 1897 the Boston Society of Arts and Crafts was founded. Its influence was far-reaching. In 1907 the National League of Handicraft Societies was constituted. There were branches in many states and a periodical, *Handicraft*, appeared, published in Montague, Massachusetts. Valuable work was done in reviving old designs and in resuscitating old methods. The New England type of crewel work was revived. Far-reaching too was the work of the Society of Blue and White Needlework in Deerfield, Massachusetts which was founded in 1896 and declared itself 'dedicated to the study and revival of a truly American type' and it gave expression to a new enthusiasm which was latent among a wide community. The Society disbanded in 1925 but the spirit which animated the Deerfield industries remains.

The parent society was the Society of Decorative Art in New York City which was formulated immediately after the English exhibition of embroideries at the Philadelphia Centennial. The objects of this Society were comprehensive and ambitious and the influence of Britain predominated.

Invaluable work has been done in the twentieth century by the Needlework and Textile Guild, Chicago, Illinois (established 1927) and the Needle and Bobbin Club, New York (established 1917).

The activities of these societies have promoted much good and progressive art in America. Outstanding too has been the influence of work by such embroiderers as Candace Wheeler and Georgiana B. Harbeson. Decorative needlework in America today is progressive, incorporating technical methods such as machine stitching and group work. The modern American embroideress, while finding inspiration in time-hallowed examples from the past, interprets the art for her own generation.

14 Modern embroidery

In an age when the machine is a powerful factor in human life, the worth of craftsmanship is increased on account of its value as a form of self-expression. The craft of embroidery has a perennial aesthetic appeal and those countries which set a value on the continuation of tradition are active in maintaining what is essentially one of the oldest crafts. Educational thought of today stresses the importance of manual dexterity alongside academic achievement for the full development of intellectual faculties. Embroidery is therefore assured a secure place in schemes of education. Much in the manner in which religion proved the main incentive in the creation of embroidery in the Middle Ages, so formal education proves an incentive to fine and ambitious work today.

The worth of crafts must be considered against the economic and social background of the age in which they are created. Embroidery work of today has to compete against machine-made imitations and products. Another factor is the scant leisure that the modern woman has for this type of work; with a multitude of interests, she is little inclined to embroider coverings for suites of furniture or wall hangings adorned with figures depicting scenes from history or mythology. The individual embroiderer seldom undertakes work on an ambitious scale today. Some fine embroideries of such a nature are, however, still created by corporate effort or in trade workshops. The 'quilting bees' or embroidery groups of the past have, in some measure, their counterpart in the groups working for churches and civic interests today. Mrs Archibald Christie in her book *Samplers and Stitches* has indicated some of the most lively opportunities for embroiderers. 'Civic functions', she says, 'may in the future give rise to new developments in embroidery. Why should not our mayors, magistrates and masters of colleges have their gowns stitched over with their symbols of office? Opportunity for the use of bold types of design and workmanship are afforded by banners and street hangings. Symbolical figures, mottoes and heraldry, executed perhaps in applied or inlaid work make suitable decoration for these.' The incentive is already there and groups of embroiderers are already taking up the challenge.

The secret of the survival of many of the older crafts lies in the fact that they concentrate on creating work which is *individual*. The successful craftsman concentrates on creating something which the machine is powerless to create and endeavours to manipulate his tools in such a manner that the machine is powerless to imitate. This does not mean that the craftsman despises the machine. At times, mechanical devices are called in to assist the craftsman but machine work is always subservient to handwork. Indeed at times the modern embroiderer creates designs (plate 84) incorporating machine work, but the hand stitchery still tends to takes precedence in artistry and charm. The modern woman introduces a personal touch to already woven apparel and to the furnishings of her home. Embroidery is at its best when it serves to fulfil an essential need; in an age when work and need are divorced, then craftsmanship deteriorates. The Victorians neglected this rule and somewhat tragically worked meticulously and diligently on specimens of no real value.

Much of the embroidery work done in the first quarter of the twentieth century took the form of copying from the work done in the seventeenth and eighteenth centuries and was in part a revolt from the trends of the nineteenth century work. Although some valuable lessons were rediscovered through this custom of copying, a tendency towards desultory work crept in; for example deliberate attempts were made to imitate colour harmonies and to match colours which time had mellowed. The workers forgot the dictum that the antique is good for inspiration but bad for slavish imitation.

Nowhere was this more apparent than in the sphere of embroidery design. The craft of embroidery has developed slowly in the past for designs were always in harmony with the life and craft of the time. There was a close freemasonry among craft workers enabling a designer, even if not a practical embroiderer, to create designs suitable for the craft. In modern times, embroidery has been subject to unstable conflicting influences due to the fact that the designer and embroiders no longer work in close proximity. Deliberate efforts have therefore been made by schools of embroidery, notably the experiment which was made by the Needlework Development Scheme, to bring together the creative artist and the technical worker. The many specimens of the Needlework Development Scheme which are now housed in the Victoria and Albert Museum, the Embroiderers' Guild and the Glasgow School of Art, are convincing evidence of the success of the effort.

Regional interest in embroidery has also produced remarkable work in a variety of forms, incorporating stitches such as feather stitch and buttonhole stitch; and combining these skilfully with good designs and colour has allied them to modern needs. Similarly Welsh quilt patterns and the intricacies of English smocks have led to new and artistic adaptations. Modern work stresses the appropriateness of the purpose and design, and the bond between these and the place where the work will be used. It stresses suitability of material, of colour, of tone and of texture; the suitability of the stitchery and the rhythm of the total effect and finish. In short the work must be justified in its aim and in the words of Selwyn Image 'the aim of the embroiderer must be not to show "see how skilful I am" but simply to make the niceties of his craft tell for the general effectiveness of the design seen at the proper distance'.

As more and more attention is being given to the need for close co-operation between designer and embroiderer, the more modern tendency there is to carry the affinity between all kinds of craftsmen further. Designers look around them to adjacent fields of art for inspiration; paintings, both ancient and modern, provide many sources of design (plate 84). As in the past, designers find woodcuts fecund material for their purpose and in like manner they study mosaic work and woven tapestries. A rich and newer source of inspiration is provided by original modern theatre decor.

The variety of embroidery which has evolved since the Second World War is characterized by the general tendency to simplification (plates 41, 45, 52), due to the expense of labour and the fact that the amateur worker's time is limited. A new approach to embroidery has come about owing to the creation of man-made fabrics such as nylon, Dacron, Terylene and materials with untarnishable threads such as Lurex (plate 82). Technical methods of handling these have advanced and new uses have been made of washable materials with gold and silver threads and also of transparent materials such as nylon. The future prospect for corporate embroidery has led to a reassessment of materials; embroidery work in harmonious colourings is highly suitable for furnishing not only the more elaborate churches (plate 39) but also the plainer, architecturally austere chapels, and modern interior designers are growing ever more conscious of the possibilities of embroidery in the home.

Considerable and deliberate efforts have been made to educate the populace in recent times in the worth and tradition of embroidery by revealing to them the beautiful work of the past and by guiding forms of expression in the present. Educational authorities encourage the development and practice of embroidery. Museums have played an important part in exhibiting in an attractive manner old needlework collected from many countries. The prejudice and apathy towards museums is slowly breaking down and this advance has been achieved in part by the excellent displays of embroidery arranged in such a manner as to meet as well as educate the taste of the populace. The Royal School of Needlework and numerous art schools have shown themselves enthusiastic, as well as sympathetic to the revival of interest in embroidery.

Glossary

Appliqué or applied work is used for bold decorative effects. The design is cut out in contrasting material and is then *applied* to the background by some simple embroidery stitch. Sometimes motifs are embroidered before being applied to the foundation material.

Inlaid appliqué Here designs are cut simultaneously out of two different fabrics, the motif of one is then inserted into the cut space of the other.

Assisi embroidery Traditional Italian embroidery, simple and decorative. The design is left unworked; the background is filled in with cross stitch. The design is outlined in double running stitch. Formal designs are usual for this work.

Berlin work Known as 'Zephyrs' in USA. Canvas embroidery, very popular in the nineteenth century. Various stitches used. Effects produced by raised work and bead work.

Black work Black silk stitchery on white linen; said to have been inspired by early printing. A variety of stitches used and the work enhanced by red silk and metallic thread.

Broderie Anglaise White embroidery; the pattern is emphasized by holes buttonholed or overcast.

Canvas work Work on counted thread but designs are often stamped on the material. Tent stitch is the most usual but a variety of stitches is used.

Crewel work Bold oriental designs, often termed Jacobean, are worked on strong fabric in coloured worsteds. Stitches are numerous with scope for artistic filling-in stitches.

Couching or laid work Threads are laid in parallel lines on the material and are then secured by small stitches worked in a thinner thread. An economic way of filling in; metallic thread is often used in this way.

Cut work An effective form of embroidery worked in buttonhole stitch. Parts of the background are cut away. The design is then thrown into relief.

In Venetian ladder work and Richelieu work, parts of the design are united by bars of buttonhole stitching, decorated with picots. Italian cut work has geometrical spaces with needlepoint fillings.

Drawn fabric work Certain warp or weft threads are removed. The remaining threads are secured with decorative stitches. Special stitches serve to draw the fabric into openwork patterns.

Florentine work Canvas embroidery. The work is sometimes called Hungarian point, fianna or flame stitch. Flame-like points are features of many designs. By the use of vertical stitches zig-zag lines in graduated tones of colour are made.

Hardanger embroidery An attractive embroidery originating in the beautiful Hardanger region on Norway's western coast. It is a form of drawn thread embroidery formed of geometrical patterns, based on square spaces. Satin stitch is used for the designs which are arranged in blocks.

Hedebo embroidery Traditional Danish work; white embroidery incorporating cut and drawn work.

Mountmellick embroidery Irish white work embroidery. A variety of stitches used but there is no open work.

Needleweaving A form of drawn thread work usually worked on coarse material. The weft threads are removed. Patterns are made on the warp threads by weaving coloured silks in and out of these threads with a needle.

Net embroidery Patterns are outlined on net. Work is often done from the back of the foundation – 'shadow work'. Lace stitches are used for fillings.

Opus Anglicanum A period of English ecclesiastical embroidery; thirteenth and fourteenth centuries. Work of a very high standard. English embroidery had at this time an international reputation. There are very many valuable specimens showing vigorous designs representing sacred scenes and figures often with an elaborate architectural background. Technique is of a very high standard. Extensive use of gold embroidery.

Orphrey Band of gold embroidery.

Patchwork Scraps of material are sewn together or mounted on unbleached calico. A template is used for cutting geometrical shapes and these are sewn with overcasting.

> *Crazy patchwork* is made up of irregularly shaped scraps of material.
> *Appliquéd patchwork* is made up of motifs cut out of scraps and applied to a foundation fabric.

Quilting Two layers of material are joined together with an interlayer of padding. Running stitch or back stitch is used to outline the pattern which is worked out with the aid of a template.

Italian quilting is a fascinating variation. A cord is threaded through two parallel lines made by running stitches, giving a raised effect to a design.

Shadow work A design is worked on the wrong side of a transparent fabric, giving a shadowy effect on the right side.

Smocking Material is gathered in pleats. These are then caught together by various fancy stitches to form a design which is often traditional to a locality. These designs vary from simple honeycombing to the most elaborate patterns.

Stump work A form of raised or padded embroidery. It was a usual characteristic of seventeenth century pictures and it was customary to use white satin.

Tambour work A small hook is used to form chain stitch embroidery. The material is held in place in a frame resembling the top of a drum.

List of museums

British

ART GALLERY AND MUSEUM Victoria Road, High Wycombe
BOWES MUSEUM Barnard Castle, County Durham
BRISTOL CITY ART GALLERY Queens Road, Bristol
BRITISH MUSEUM Gt Russell Street, London WC1
CHURCH PORCH FOLK MUSEUM Winchcombe, Glos.
CITY ART GALLERY Mosley Street, Manchester
CITY MUSEUM AND ART GALLERY Nottingham
FERENS ART GALLERY City Square, Hull
GEORGIAN HOUSE Great George Street, Bristol
HONITON AND ALL HALLOWS MUSEUM Honiton
HOVE MUSEUM OF ART New Church Road, Hove
LONDON MUSEUM Kensington Palace, London, W8
MUSEUM AND MONUMENT ROOM Castle Acre, Guildford
MUSEUM AND ART GALLERY Wardown Park, Luton
PRIEST'S HOUSE West Hoathly, Sussex
ROYAL SCOTTISH MUSEUM Edinburgh 1
RUSHOLME GALLERY OF ENGLISH COSTUME Manchester
SOMERSET COUNTY MUSEUM Taunton Castle, Taunton
THORPE PREBEND HOUSE Ripon, Yorks
VICTORIA AND ALBERT MUSEUM South Kensington, London, SW7
WELSH FOLK MUSEUM St Fagans, South Wales
WERNHER COLLECTION Luton Hoo

American

AMERICAN-SWEDISH INSTITUTE Minneapolis, Minn.
ART INSTITUTE OF CHICAGO Chicago, Ill.
BROOKLYN MUSEUM Brooklyn N.Y.
CINCINNATI ART MUSEUM Cincinnati, Ohio
CLEVELAND MUSEUM OF ART Cleveland, Ohio
COLONIAL WILLIAMSBURG Williamsburg, Va.
COOPER HEWITT MUSEUM New York, N.Y.
DAUGHTERS OF THE AMERICAN REVOLUTION NATIONAL SOCIETY MUSEUM Washington, D.C.
DENVER ART MUSEUM Denver, Colo.
DETROIT INSTITUTE OF ARTS Detroit, Mich.
THE METROPOLITAN MUSEUM OF ART New York, N.Y.
MUSEUM OF THE CITY OF NEW YORK N.Y.
MUSEUM OF FINE ARTS Boston, Mass.
PHILADELPHIA MUSEUM OF ART Philadelphia, Pa.
SCALAMANDRE MUSEUM OF TEXTILES New York, N.Y.
TEXTILE MUSEUM Washington, D.C.
VIRGINIA MUSEUM OF FINE ARTS Richmond, Va.
WINTERTHUR MUSEUM Wilmington, Del.

Bibliography

BOSSERT, H. T. *Peasant Art of Europe and Asia* Zwemmer, London, 1959; and Praeger, New York, 1969

Catalogue of English Ecclesiastical Embroideries 13th-16th Centuries Victoria and Albert Museum Publications, H.M.S.O., London, 1930

CAVE, O. *English Folk Embroidery* Mills & Boon, London, 1965; and Taplinger, New York, 1966

CHRISTENSEN, E. O. *The Index of American Design* Macmillan, New York, 1950

CHRISTIE, A. H. *Samplers and Stitches: a Handbook of the Embroiderer's Art* Batsford, London, 1959

DAVENPORT, C. *English Embroidered Bindings* Routledge & Kegan Paul, London, 1899

Encyclopaedia Britannica 1967 edition

FAIRHOLT, F. W. *Costume in England* ed. Viscount Dillon, 2 vols, Bell, London, 1896

FOX-DAVIES, A. C. *Complete Guide to Heraldry* Nelson, London, 1925

HARBESON, G. B. *American Needlework* Bonanza Books, New York, 1938

HOPE, W. ST JOHN *Heraldry for Craftsmen and Designers* Hogg, London, 1913; and Macmillan, New York, 1913

HUNTON, W. G. *Decorative English Textiles* Tiranti, London, 1930

JOURDAIN, M. *English Secular Embroidery* Routledge & Kegan Paul, London, 1912; and Dutton, New York 1912

KENDRICK, A. F. *English Embroidery* Batsford, London, 1932

KING, BUCKY *Creative Canvas Embroidery* Hearthside. New York, 1967

KING, D. *Samplers* Victoria and Albert Museum Publications, H.M.S.O., London, 1968

KINMOND, J. *Anchor Book of European Embroidery* Branford, Newton Center, Mass.

KOHLER, E. 'Embroidery as an Expression of National Characteristics' *Journal of the Royal Society of Arts* vol. XCV

MACKAIL, J. W. *Life of William Morris* 2 vols, Oxford University Press, 1950; and Blom, New York, 1968

NORRIS, H. *Costume and Fashion* 2 vols, Dent, London, 1924-1938

PLANCHE, J. R. *History of English Costume to the Close of the 18th Century* Bell, London, 1900

POWER, E. *Mediaeval English Nunneries* Cambridge University Press, 1936; and Biblo & Tannen Inc., New York, 1922

RISLEY, C. *Creative Embroidery* Studio Vista, London, 1969; and Watson-Guptill Publications, New York 1969

SCHUETTE, M., and MULLER-CHRISTENSEN, S. *Pictorial History of Embroidery* Praeger, New York, 1964

STAPLEY *Popular Weaving and Embroidery in Spain* Batsford, London, 1924

WHEELER, C. *Development of Embroidery in America* Harper & Row, New York, 1921

WHITE, A. V. *Blackwork Embroidery of Today* Taplinger, New York, 1962

Index

(Plate numbers are indicated by italic figures)